Children and
Challenging Behavior

Making Inclusion Work

Children and Challenging Behavior

Making Inclusion Work

VOLUME 1

Edited by

Cindy Croft & Deborah Hewitt

CENTER FOR INCLUSIVE CHILD CARE

2010

Printed and bound in the United States.
First edition, 2004
Second edition, 2010

LCCN: 2004103351
ISBN: 0-9719304-4-9

Designed and typeset by Judy Gilats, St. Paul

Quantity discounts are available for organizations or universities. Contact:
Center for Inclusive Child Care
275 N. Syndicate St.
St. Paul, MN 55104
www.inclusivechildcare.org
croft@csp.edu

Contents

Acknowledgments

Volumes 1 and 2 of *Children and Challenging Behavior: Making Inclusion Work* represent the efforts of a dedicated group that includes Center for Inclusive Child Care (CICC) trainers, state department personnel, parents, early childhood professionals, special educators and college instructors. The body of work represents years of collective wisdom and practice in including children with special needs in community child care settings. It is with gratitude and appreciation that we acknowledge these individuals for their contributions to both the first and second editions.

Support
Barbara O'Sullivan and Michael Eastman for their constant commitment to supporting a system of inclusive child care through the CICC. Their leadership, wisdom, and compassion have helped frame the work done by the CICC. Christine Bentley for her ongoing contribution to the work of the CICC.

Editing
Debbie Hewitt for her great skill in editing, writing, and rewriting. Her keen eye for both content and detail enabled the CICC to produce an incredibly well written resource for teaching about children and their behaviors. She also wrote a *Writer's Guide* for authors to follow which served as an excellent tool.

Writers
Each author was chosen because of her expertise in early childhood behavior guidance. They were all given the task to write a specific chapter that would eventually mesh with other chapters into a whole that would support child care practitioners doing inclusive child care.

Contributors

Sherry Haaf, Kristen Wheeler, and LuAnn Olen contributed the foundation to this present work.

Design and Typesetting

Judy Gilats for her skill in changing a manuscript into a book.

Photographer

Keri Pickett for her wonderful pictures of children.

Introduction

"Because they are children
and for no other reason,
they have dignity and respect,
simply because they are."

Barbara Coloroso

THIS quote speaks to the philosophy of the Center for Inclusive Child Care (CICC) whose mission is to be a centralized, comprehensive resource network supporting inclusive care for children in community settings. The Center for Inclusive Child Care was named in 2001 as a result of broadening the scope of work formerly done by Project EXCEPTIONAL, which began as a state-funded inclusion training program developed by Sonoma State University with the California Department of Education. Sonoma State University replicated the training model in Minnesota through a training grant from the federal Office of Special Education and Rehabilitation Services in Washington, D.C., to recruit and educate child care providers on how to include children with disabilities in community child care settings. The Center for Inclusive Child Care is funded today with support from the Minnesota Departments of Human Services and Education, the McKnight Foundation, and other revenue sources.

In January of 1996, 11 multi-disciplinary teams from communities across Minnesota attended the Project EXCEPTIONAL Training of Trainer workshop series by Sonoma State University staff and funded jointly by Minnesota Departments of Human Services and Education. Over the next few years, a more diverse pool of trainers was added across the state as community training needs arose. These teams are a critical link for recruiting and training child care and development staff for young children with special needs throughout the state.

As training was provided and practitioners began to implement what they learned, the need for additional supports and new topics in training were identified. The Center for Inclusive Child Care is now affiliated with the College of Education at Concordia University, St. Paul, Minnesota. As part of the services to support inclusive child care, development of an inclusion consultation model, additional training components, and the website www.inclusivechildcare.org were added.

As part of the CICC system of support, *Children and Challenging Behaviors: Making Inclusion Work* was designed to meet the increasing needs of early childhood and school-age practitioners providing care for children with behavior challenges.

Core Philosophies of the Center for Inclusive Child Care

A core belief of the CICC is that all children are children first. Children need to be seen in the context of the whole child, not just the special need. When challenging behaviors arise, it is sometimes difficult to separate the behavior from the child. It is important that practitioners understand what the function of the behavior is for the child so they can accommodate that special need in an individual way. The function of behavior is a concept explained in chapter four of Volume 1.

A second core belief is that all children have a right to belong in all community settings. The Center for Inclusive Child Care is committed to providing support to early childhood and school-age practitioners so they can successfully include children with special needs in their programs. To that end, the CICC has developed *Children and Challenging Behaviors: Making Inclusion Work, Volumes 1 and 2*, in order that quality training can be provided for practitioners around issues of children's behavior. Volume 1 contains a series of monographs that describe the basis for children's behaviors and strategies for including children whose behaviors are challenging. Volume 2 is a series of training activities that reflect the content of each chapter of Volume 1.

Another philosophy that guides this work is that inclusion of children with and without special needs benefits all children. Research supports inclusion as sound developmentally appropriate practice (Allen, Cowdery, 2008). All children learn in a social context that is enriched when their peers are typically and atypically developing.

The Center for Inclusive Child Care is also committed to inclusive, supportive language. In addition to adhering to child first language, the CICC believes that the language describing a special need is important. Issues around behavior need to be articulated in language that is nonjudgmental and objective. For example, in the text, "guiding" behavior replaces "managing" behavior. Children are not seen as "challenging" or difficult, rather their behaviors may challenge practitioners. Changing the way language is used can change attitudes about some of the behaviors that may be presented by children, with or without a special need.

In addition, intervention is used in the text to describe both a formal and an informal activity. The distinction between formal and informal intervention is in the way it is conducted and its purpose. An informal assessment is done by an early childhood or school-age practitioner through observation and recording of daily activities of children in their program. The informal assessment is used to adapt programming to meet individual learning needs and may be helpful in relating to a parent about a child's development. An informal assessment by an early childhood or school-age practitioner might lead a parent to local resources for a screening or formal assessment. Professionals in special education, mental health, or the medical profession might conduct the formal assessment. There are a variety of methods used in formal assessment, including testing, interviews, observation, and medical examination. The relationship between formal and informal assessment is important because it may be the informal assessment by the practitioner that leads a parent to seek a formal assessment in order to receive services for their child's special need.

Finally, the CICC believes in building on the individual strengths of early childhood and school-age practitioners by offering support and resources, including training opportunities. Inclusive child care is not optional; it is required under the Americans with Disabilities Act. Therefore, the CICC is committed to developing and coordinating services for practitioners that will encourage their success in caring for children with special needs.

Explanation of Layout of Materials

Children and Challenging Behaviors: Making Inclusion Work was developed to provide support to early childhood and school-age practitioners through training and educational opportunities around the behavioral needs of children. It is a holistic approach that helps practitioners examine their role in behavior, as well as the role of environment, temperament, and disability.

Children and Challenging Behaviors: Making Inclusion Work is designed in two volumes. Volume 1 is a collection of monographs written by authors from across the United States and from a variety of backgrounds. Those backgrounds include: parent of a child with a disability, center child care, higher education, early childhood special education, and public education. Each author offers a unique perspective when looking at the behaviors that often challenge the people who work with children. Each chapter supports the core philosophies of CICC and follows a similar layout using an introduction, research-based information, and a set of key points. The training activities that follow each chapter in Volume 2 are derived from the key points in Volume 1.

Volume 1 is designed to provide a thorough understanding of the topic area so that trainers and educators can implement the training activities in Volume 2 with a degree of knowledge and expertise. Volume 1 sets the framework for workshops and classes taught from the Volume 2 activities.

In Volume 1, efforts were made to be gender fair by alternating the use of he/she in different chapters. The word "practitioner" was used to describe the diverse group of people who work with young people in many different settings. "She" was used when referring to practitioners since the majority are women. Any names that are used in Volumes 1 and 2 are fictional and examples are a composite of experiences of the authors.

In Volume 2, the CICC uses research-based adult learning methods in the presentation of training. Activity-based, experiential learning is a key component to training offered through the CICC. The presentation of workshops is strength-based and builds on what the practitioner already knows and has experienced. This supports the core belief of the CICC that practitioners already have many skills to provide care for children with special needs; they often need to build on those skills in order to be more effective.

Each chapter in Volume 2 contains several training activities that may be combined into a workshop. Each activity has a purpose and outcome statement and concludes with key points. Activities are designed to teach the core concepts through a variety of adult learning methods, such as small group to large group feedback, role play, video presentation, case studies, and strategy building. Workshops may be designed to meet an audience's training needs. In addition, workshops can be adapted by the trainer or educator in their length, scope, and age grouping of children being served.

Systems Change

The Center for Inclusive Child Care is committed to changing attitudes about the inclusion of children with special needs into community settings by giving practitioners the tools to be successful. Many parents have told stories of their child being refused early childhood or school-age services or expelled from child care because of the child's special need. One parent relayed the following event: The mother called her local Child Care Resource and Referral agency to find child care for her 3-year-old child, whom she said had been asked to leave thirteen early education programs because of behavior issues. When she told her son that she was going to find a new child care provider who would love him very much because he was so special, he looked at her with tears and said, "I know, mom, I'm special needs." At 3, a young child had already been faced with so much failure as part of a system that was not equipped to meet his unique learning and behavior needs. The CICC believes that with resources and professional development opportunities, early childhood and school-age practitioners can successfully include children with behavior challenges into their settings.

REFERENCES

Allen, K. Eileen and Cowdery, Glynnis. (2008). *The Exceptional Child: Inclusion in Early Childhood Education*. Delmar: Albany, NY.

Coloroso, Barbara. *Winning at Parenting*. Kids are Worth It. (1989).

Project EXCEPTONAL: *A Guide to Training and Recruiting Child Care Providers to Serve Young Children with Disabilities*. (1996). California Department of Education: Sacramento.

PART 1

Developmentally Appropriate Practice: Understanding Children and Their Behavior

CHAPTER 1

Children's Behavior:
The Importance
of the Practitioner's Role

Deborah Hewitt & Lynn Gehrke

Introduction

TAYLOR and David are in the block area crouched over the train tracks. They have divided the cars to the train between themselves and are working to connect the tracks. Sam enters the room and calls out "Teacher, I'm gonna play with the train." He takes off his coat and runs to the block area. He wedges himself into the small spot between Taylor and David and helps himself to three of the cars. As he begins to tear the tracks apart, he says in a loud voice, to no one in particular, "This doesn't go here, it goes over there."

Taylor and David demand the return of the cars, but Sam clutches them tightly to his chest. He starts to bounce on his knees and sobs, "They're mine. You can't have them." The teacher arrives on the scene and Sam continues to sob. As the teacher sorts out what happened, Sam is asked to return the cars. Instead, he throws one to the ground and stomps on it. The teacher reminds Sam of the rule to take care of the toys and tells him to find somewhere he could play more calmly. He continues to complain loudly and stamp his feet. Finally, he falls to the floor and buries his face in his hands. Taylor and David move to another part of the room.

Early childhood practitioners face situations like these each day. They wonder about the best way to respond to an episode like Sam's and other behaviors that can be difficult to handle. They question how to respond when a child is physical toward others, demands an inordinate amount of attention, has emotional outbursts, or refuses to do what adults ask.

These and other behaviors can be perplexing to adults. It is through their behaviors that children ask the adults around them for help expressing strong emotions, learning to get along with others, and learning to cope with the disappointments or pain they experience. How do "intentional" early childhood practitioners respond to these requests? What would they do when working with a child whose behavior challenges them to teach a new behavior?

A great deal of thought goes into the decisions a practitioner makes about intentional approaches to challenging behaviors. Decisions must be based on sound theoretical information about social and emotional development. Practitioners need to fully understand developmentally appropriate expectations and how the child's behavior fits within them. Early childhood practitioners observe to learn the child's current level of development, strengths, areas in which growth is needed, and the child's unique style of learning. The practitioners' observations also help them learn what times of day or types of activities might upset a child. They learn to recognize the signs and anticipate situations that frustrate a child and then offer support.

Accomplished practitioners consider the effect that environment has on children. After arranging the environment, practitioners make any necessary adaptations so each child can be as independent as possible. The practitioner allows opportunities throughout the day for children to make choices and control their own play. They understand how to bring children together to form a sense of community and to build relationships with each other.

Working with children who demonstrate challenging behaviors requires that practitioners use a wide variety of strategies that will help a child learn inner control and problem-solving skills. Practitioners carefully choose from among the many strategies they know and match the most effective approach to the needs of the individual. They also recognize that one strategy might not work for long and what was successful once might not be a second time. They are aware that a strategy that helped one child might not be the best for another one. They strive to learn about each child's situation, abilities, and disabilities.

A great deal of patience, understanding, and knowledge is needed when working with children who have emotional and behavioral needs. To stay positive about children's behaviors, practitioners take care of themselves to reduce stress and stay healthy. They make an effort to have positive connections outside of the classroom (2004, Gartrell). Even the most experienced practitioners realize that they must be lifelong learners and seek information about the difficult behaviors they face. They take classes, read information, and learn from others as they make every effort to further develop and improve their own skills.

Early childhood practitioners have the opportunity to have an impact on the lives of the children they touch. That positive impact develops out of positive relationships with children and their families. When a practitioner develops a strong relationship that is built on acceptance and respect, she provides a child with hope for success now and in the future. Through a caring relationship, a child feels appreciated and valued. Many children can withstand challenges if they have a relationship with an adult who deeply cares about them, believes in their potential, and believes in their ability to prevail.

Many Behaviors Pose Challenges

There are many behaviors in the early years that demonstrate to practitioners that children are struggling and need to learn new behaviors. These children often are frustrated, withdrawn, boisterously physical and verbal, or non-compliant.

For instance, some children have life experiences and neurological challenges that create greater emotional needs. A child who is experiencing life stresses that are beyond her ability to cope might demonstrate her frustration, confusion, and sadness through her behaviors.

She might have difficulty concentrating, finding it hard to focus or become involved in play. She might move from one activity to another, merely touching the materials without becoming actively engaged. As her attention flits from one group of children to another, she might enter their play briefly, sometimes being more disruptive than playful. In addition, it might be extremely difficult for a child with these behaviors to make decisions. She might not be able to focus on two choices. She might look for a third option or she may fluctuate back and forth without making a decision.

Another child might express pent up frustration and anger by lashing out. She may be physical toward children and adults alike. Biting, hitting, pushing, pulling another's hair, or spitting are all physical behaviors that a child might demonstrate if she has few other ways to express herself. These behaviors are not only dangerous but are usually upsetting to all involved.

Explosive outbursts and uncontrollable floods of emotion can also be a part of the challenging behaviors that early childhood practitioners face. A child with few internal controls could feel overwhelmed by her own emotions. She might not have developed the ability to express herself in more constructive ways or to tell people how much she is hurting. She has an inability to pause between having an impulse to act and carrying through with the action.

Avoiding conflicts, being uncommunicative, and withdrawing from relationships might also be ways in which a child tells adults that she is having trouble coping. This child might choose activities that isolate her such as doing puzzles or working at the easel. She might be reluctant to participate in activities, avoid eye contact, or refuse to answer questions. Social interactions can be extremely painful for this child. This child may be in a group experience for the first time, or extremely shy and unable to trust the situation, children, or adults.

One practitioner may find the physical acting out of a child extremely frustrating, another the way a child withdraws from activities, and another, the outbursts of a tantruming child. The internal voice a practitioner hears might reflect that her buttons have been pushed by this behavior or situation. A frustrated practitioner might hear herself think, "That kid is always making trouble." Practitioners need to identify which behaviors are the most upsetting to them and learn to calm down, reframe the behavior, and effectively deal with the situation at hand. Hyson suggests "refocusing" the emotion in order to help children learn to talk about and use their emotions in a culturally and developmentally appropriate manner (Hyson, 2004).

Mary Sheedy Kurcinka in her book, *Raising Your Spirited Child* (2006), describes how labels can affect our perception of a challenging behavior. If a child is considered a troublemaker, a problem child, or a kid who is out to get you, a person might respond to these negative descriptors and treat the child accordingly. "Crabby Abby" becomes just that, because this is what people expect from her. "The biter" continues to bite. Because the people around her have been so frustrated, they have not yet taught her more appropriate ways to deal with her frustration. They see her behavior instead of her distinctive characteristics and the strengths she possesses. By focusing only on the biting behavior, practitioners miss the child's obvious request for help in expressing her needs and emotions in a way that doesn't hurt others. How a child is labeled or the view that a practitioner has of her affects how the practitioner responds. Practitioners need to guard against labeling a child difficult or challenging. Instead, they should reframe the situation or look at the same situation from a different perspective (Hewitt and Heidemann, 2002). Reframing helps practitioners see challenging behaviors in new ways. Rather than viewing a child who asks the same question over-and-over again as tiresome, regard her persistence as a strength that will eventually help her complete homework. An anxious child might be considered as cautious, an explosive child as dramatic, and a nosy child as curious (Kurcinka, 2006). These new ways of viewing the child's behavior help practitioners focus on the positive and reach a new level of understanding and appreciation. As the practitioner's perspective changes, so does the way in which she treats the child. The practitioner can refocus her thoughts by thinking, "What does this child need to learn from me at this moment?"

Practitioners Take on Many Roles

There are many roles that a practitioner takes on as she tries to support the growth and development of a child. She becomes a detective, looking for clues about influences on a child's behavior. The practitioner acts as a guide by helping a child learn to interact with others. She serves as a role model when children observe her actions and learn ways of coping with feelings, dealing with frustration, and getting along with others. Above all else, a practitioner nurtures the children around her by promoting their development and fostering positive relationships.

The practitioner nurtures each child with whom she works by accepting each one for who they are. She values each child as a unique individual. Learning about the child's abilities and understanding the path of development allow the practitioner to nourish the child's growth by matching learning opportunities to her needs. She supports the child's progress, assumes there will be setbacks, and believes in the child's ability to grow toward her potential.

As a guide, the practitioner recognizes that learning the complex skills needed to get along with others takes many years. The practitioner offers choices that help to steer the child toward appropriate activities. When conflicts occur, the practitioner teaches ways to resolve the issue and discusses with the child ways that a similar upset might be avoided in the future. As the practitioner guides play it helps facilitate interactions between play partners. Through guidance, a practitioner leads the way for a child to develop appropriate behavior and social skills.

The model that the practitioner offers is powerful. Observing others is one of the most significant ways in which children learn. The way a practitioner expresses feelings, demonstrates the ability to solve problems, and interacts in kind and caring ways are lessons that children absorb. Particularly important are the lessons that the practitioner demonstrates about how to treat others. In interactions with adults and children alike, the practitioner needs to model listening, acceptance of differences, consideration for another person's feelings, and ways to offer help. A practitioner can help children learn about positive social interactions by demonstrating them in relationships.

Children bring to the early childhood setting a birth history, physical abilities and disabilities, a family context, past triumphs and failures, and experiences with other caregivers. The practitioner learns a great deal from direct observations of the child. Watching him play with other children, approach difficult situations, cope with challenges, and deal with his emotions will provide the practitioner with a number of clues about the most effective ways to respond to his needs.

In addition, a practitioner will want to gather information from other sources. It is essential to build a relationship with family members and learn about their culture as well as their parenting style. This information can lead to greater understanding and consistency between home and the early childhood setting. Accumulating information from specialists that may be involved in a child's care is also vital in providing the most appropriate care. Not only must a practitioner be fully aware of any special needs a child might have, but she must also be an active partner in designing and implementing a plan for care and education. A practitioner takes on the role of detective and accumulates all the pertinent information, analyzes it, draws conclusions, and develops a plan for success.

Factors That Can Influence Behavior

As the practitioner observes and learns about a child, some of the factors that influence the child's behavior may be discovered. There are many factors that can affect a child's social interactions or ability to cope with frustrations, change, or disappointments. Some of these are external factors that are part of a child's environment, either at home or in the early childhood setting. Some are internal factors that might have a neurological base. Some factors can be controlled, reducing the tension for the child. Others are difficult or impossible to control. A child might need to be taught and re-taught to cope with the factors that are outside of her control (Poulsen, 1996).

External Factors That Might Influence a Child's Behavior
▶ An environment that is overstimulating
▶ Expectations that are too high or too low
▶ Feeling crowded
▶ Witnessing or being a victim of abuse (sexual, physical, or emotional)
▶ Neglect
▶ Activities that demand too little or too much

► Inconsistent expectations
► Loss of a loved one
► Addition of a sibling
► Arguments with a caregiver or between parents
► Infrequent opportunities to make choices
► Medication
► Being encouraged or rewarded for aggression
► Exposure to media violence
► Frequent changes in caregivers or routines
► Unmet emotional needs
► Poverty or worries about money
► Mental illness of parent or family member
► Substance abuse by family member

Internal Factors That Might Influence a Child's Behavior
► Temperament
► Illness
► Fatigue
► Hunger
► Poor nutrition
► Physical disabilities
► Neurological challenges
► Developmental lags
► Speech and language difficulties

Additional known and unknown factors might cause distress for a child. When a factor can be identified, it might be possible to eliminate or modify it, thereby reducing the stress the child experiences.

For example, if a child is hungry when he arrives at child care, it may help him play more calmly and be ready to learn if he has breakfast or a snack. Sometimes, programs or practitioners will reject this suggestion because they might feel breakfast is the parent's responsibility or that it would take too much work or require a change in schedule. However, each child's basic needs must be met before he can be expected to work and play with other children in a cooperative manner. Practitioners need flexibility in their programs and a willingness to do whatever is needed to help a child perform at his best.

Other Changes that Might be Within the Practitioner's Control
▶ Offer developmentally appropriate activities
▶ Provide choices
▶ Work with the parents to develop consistent expectations and consequences
▶ Attend to the child before challenging behavior occurs
▶ Reduce stimulation in the early childhood setting
▶ Give the child large spaces in which to work and play
▶ Talk with the parent about medications and understand all side effects
▶ Turn off the TV in your setting
▶ Strive for consistency in caregivers
▶ Establish routines
▶ Arrange additional services such as speech and language therapy

Practitioners sometimes become frustrated if they want to change factors that are outside of their control. For example, it is unlikely that many families will turn off the TV or forbid their child to watch superhero programs. If the practitioner and the family disagree about certain practices, complaining does little. Instead, the practitioner should focus on family strengths and create situations in which the child can succeed by controlling factors within the early childhood setting.

Building Relationship

The relationship developed with a child is the foundation upon which a child's sense of security is built. Children thrive when they are in trusting, loving, respectful relationships. Through a child's earliest relationships, she learns to be trusting or fearful. If a child experiences adults who are nurturing, she learns that those around her will keep her safe and help to settle her when she feels out of control. A child learns that adults will help her to develop inner controls and learn to live within the rules. Relationships that are caring and affectionate help a child believe that she is worthy of love and attention. The relationships she builds with her caregivers are the blueprints for all other relationships.

Some children have a temperament that draws people to them. They tend to be sociable, cheerful, outgoing, communicative, and approachable. Entering into a relationship with others is more difficult because they could be shy, withdrawn, unkempt, argumentative, bossy, aggressive, or fussy. Regardless of their disposition or the challenging behaviors they present, each child has strengths and qualities that make her unique. Practitioners must look beneath the surface and begin to appreciate some of the qualities that make each child endearing.

The teacher-child relationship is the responsibility of the teacher. It is the teacher's responsibility to build it and nurture it. Building a relationship with a child takes time and effort. It takes weeks and months to cultivate a mutual bond. As people spend time with one another, they build a history including activities, experiences, and memories.

To begin to build a relationship, a practitioner must start with the basics. Determine the child's likes and dislikes. What are her favorite things to eat, play, and do? Surprise her with her favorites. Watch to see what this child does well. Recognize these strengths and find ways for her to build on them. Learn about the child's family, their customs, activities, and routines. Reflect the familiar in the early childhood setting. It is especially important to develop a cooperative relationship with the child's family. The child will sense this positive regard for those she loves and absorb it.

Be certain the schedule allows adequate time for less-structured activities. Child initiated activities provides time for relationship building. Sit with a child as she plays. Let the child decide the direction of play and follow her lead. Comment on things she does by saying something like, "Now you're stacking the red one on top of the blue." Spending time together validates a child's play and helps her feel valued.

Encourage a child to develop trust by being trustworthy. Responding to a child's physical and emotional needs is essential. If she needs to rest, find a way to let her sleep. Feed her when she is hungry instead of when the clock suggests that it is time for lunch. Help her calm down when she is overexcited and regain her composure when she is out of control. Follow through on promises as well as consequences that are stated. Tell a child about your movements and your touch. For example, "I'm going to wheel your chair closer to the table. Then you can reach the toys."

When challenging behaviors occur, a consistent, caring, positive relationship will enable the teacher to help the child, because the child trusts the teacher. Sometimes, a troublesome behavior improves for a while, but then resurfaces. One contributing factor could be that a strong relationship is not being maintained. Once a relationship is established, it cannot be ignored. For a relationship to flourish, it must be maintained with time and attention. Rebuild the relationship, paying particular attention to the strengths of the child.

JARENE was finding it especially difficult to get close to Sarah. From the time Sarah joined her home child care, she tried to take control of the children's play and hoard materials. She often told children the rules but did not follow them herself. She also ignored directions or did the opposite and did not listen when Jarene tried to explain something. To make it even more difficult to get close, Sarah often had a runny nose and sometimes was so dirty that she smelled bad.

Jarene realized that she needed to build a strong relationship with Sarah. She knew a positive relationship would help Sarah learn to trust her, spur cooperation, and Sarah might test her less often. In an effort to find Sarah's strengths, Jarene watched her more closely for the next few days. One day, Sarah decorated a strip of paper, stapled it into a ring and glued sparkling confetti to it. Soon she was teaching other children and patiently helping them construct their own crowns. The next day Sarah bent over her work at the table. She made marks in rows across her paper, until the paper was full. Then she stood up, held the paper in front of her and sang the song she had invented. Finally she announced, "I'm like Beethoven."

Jarene came to recognize Sarah's creativity and ability to share her ideas with others. Without making a specific effort to look for Sarah's positive characteristics, Jarene may not have noticed these qualities so quickly. ✸

Responsive Care Builds Feelings of Self-Worth

Everyday the interactions a child has with others either enhances or diminishes her feelings of self-worth. The messages that a child hears can build or destroy a child's developing sense of self. Harsh responses, put downs, and threats can tear away at a child's feelings of competence and confidence. Children who lack high levels of self-esteem are less likely to try new things, approach another child with confidence, or might take a passive role in arguments. Children with low self-esteem may also hurt themselves or others, become easily frustrated, and could find it more difficult to tolerate even low levels of stress.

Children do best when they hear messages that support their emerging sense of self. Affirmations such as "I'm glad you are in my group" help a child feel as if she belongs. Affirming a child's feelings can help her feel understood. She might feel accepted when she hears "It's okay to feel sad. I feel sad when I say good-bye to my mom, too."

Placing positive expectations on the child's behavior sets up a self-fulfilling prophecy that says you believe she will do the right thing. A child is likely to respond in the way expected when a practitioner says something like, "She wants to look at your toy and then I'm sure she will give it right back."

All children feel better about themselves when someone acknowledges the things that they do well. Giving children messages about appropriate behaviors help build their level of esteem. All messages about a child's behavior should be given in a one-on-one conversation. Recognition that is broadcast to the group could seem insincere or manipulative. It generally means a lot more to the individual if a practitioner moves close to her, gets down on her eye level, and speaks specifically about the behavior. The tone of voice and body language of the practitioner carries a strong message too. Be sure to use a pleasant tone, and relaxed mannerisms when giving positive messages. A child can feel a sense of pride when her caregiver bends down to her, places a hand on her shoulder, and says, in an appreciative tone, "Thank you for helping to pick up the doll clothes. There sure were a lot of them." Feedback about a child's newly developing ability to share might sound something like, "You and Pa Ying both wanted the clipboard. I see you decided she would have it first and, then, you. You are really learning to share." A child with challenging behaviors needs to hear positive messages frequently to help counter some of the responses she might receive from others.

Examining Messages from the Past

Practitioners often respond to children's behaviors in the same ways that their behaviors were treated when they were growing up. Some of these responses might have been effective and helped develop the skills needed to be competent and confident. Messages that helped a practitioner grow to be caring, understanding, and strong are worth repeating. Messages that help to build self-esteem include:

> *You're learning.*
> *I trust you.*
> *I'm glad you're here.*
> *That was so smart.*
> *I'm listening.*
> *Thanks for your help.*

Other responses that practitioners might have experienced could leave a person feeling devalued, unloved, or unworthy. When children are punished physically, yelled at, lectured, or belittled for inappropriate behavior they may feel like a failure, feel unworthy of love or attention, feel angry or embarrassed, and may learn to distrust adults. Messages that work to destroy self-esteem include:

> *Here, let me do it.*
> *Don't be such a baby.*
> *You're a spoiled brat.*
> *Shame on you!*
> *I don't care what you want.*
> *Shut up!*

While punitive experiences and negative messages might be a part of a practitioner's past, they can acknowledge them and decide not to repeat them. It is possible for practitioners with this background to learn more supportive ways to respond, more appropriate ways to express their own anger and frustration, and how to problem-solve in a variety of situations. This requires a great deal of self-awareness. Practitioners must first recognize the messages they heard while growing up, acknowledge the ones they are repeating, and change the ones that are destructive. As practitioners interact, they need to: learn to hear their own voices; reflect on the quality of the interaction; consider the effect it may have on a child; and determine which messages are most instructional, most supportive and most caring. These messages should be said over and over.

When messages that are not supportive are said, practitioners can anticipate that a similar situation is likely to occur in the future, either with the same child or another. Practitioners must reject the negative messages they may have learned and prepare the words that will be used or a strategy to try in the future. For example, Kayla, a child care teacher, reflected on a conflict she mediated and heard herself say "If you can't share, I'm putting the toy away," a phrase that she and her sisters heard many times as they were growing up. However, Kayla remembered learning in a guiding behavior class, that if you put the toy away, you remove the opportunity for the children to learn how to get along. She knew that there would be another upset over sharing in the future and she vowed to help the children work it out. She thought through her response and decided that the next time, she would ask the children to come up with two or three ways in which they could use the toy together and then help them get started with their best idea.

All practitioners will feel their own anger well up periodically. When practitioners begin to feel angry, they need to take a moment to compose themselves before acting. If their own emotions are in check, they can guide a child more effectively. It is okay for a practitioner to let a child know that she is upset as long as the child's growing sense of self is kept as the priority. This way, a practitioner will not lose herself in her own anger. Approach the child calmly, use an "I statement" and describe why you are angry. Say something like, "I don't like it when you throw the sand out of the sand box. It makes the floor slippery and is a big mess to clean up." Work with the child to clean up and then be sure to help the child re-engage in an appropriate activity.

Practitioners act as powerful models for children. The ways they express themselves and solve their problems are often imitated by children. Relearning appropriate ways to express anger, frustration, or sadness helps teach children more acceptable ways to express themselves.

Teach Appropriate Expression of Emotions

Teaching children with emotional and behavioral needs to express their emotions in appropriate ways helps them become full participants and accepted members of their early childhood community. Practitioners can help children learn that feelings must be respected and accepted, while certain expressions of those feelings cannot.

Some children might lack the vocabulary or ability to communicate their feelings. Labeling feelings for a child can help her feel understood and can offer a sense of relief. One day at child care, when it was time for the children to get ready to go home, Khalil was asked to put on his coat. For a few minutes, he did everything but go near his locker. He wandered around the room touching the blocks, the puzzles, the easel, and the books. When his teacher took him by the hand and led him to his locker, he refused to put on his coat. She held his coat out to help him and he knocked it to the floor. Then, he climbed into the locker and held on to the hooks as tightly as he could. His teacher guessed at what he might be feeling and said, "It seems like you're sad about leav-

ing the toys to go home. You can come back tomorrow and play again." With that, Khalil climbed out of his locker and picked up the coat. He asked, "Will the sand still be in the sandbox?" As they walked to the bus together, his teacher reassured him that the sand and all the toys would still be there.

Khalil could not use words to tell his teacher about his concern. His behavior suggested that he was avoiding leaving school. With reassurance that he could come back the following day, Khalil became more compliant. Perhaps, if Khalil could have expressed his disappointment, this confrontation could have been avoided.

Practitioners need to teach children a variety of feeling words to express themselves. Mad, sad, happy, scared, and surprised are among the basics. Also, help children recognize the different intensities of their emotions. Feelings of anger can range from upset or frustrated to really, really angry. Children will need repeated practice of vocabulary or alternative methods for communicating appropriate expressions of their emotions.

When a child is angry, help her learn some appropriate ways to express her feelings. Teach her to yell "stop" or "mine." Ask her to go to an adult for help when she feels mad. Encourage her to stomp her foot to emphasize her point. Let her paint or color as an acceptable way to express her anger. Redirect her energy to a sensory activity such as play-dough or water play. Or give her a sponge ball to throw into a basket. Accept her feelings but do not allow her to hurt others or herself.

It can be frightening to other children when one child is yelling or crying. It helps if children are reminded of times when they were upset. Children come to realize that everyone experiences feelings, although the intensity with which they are expressed or the way they are expressed can differ. Help children accept a distraught child's feelings, respond to another's signals of distress, and, when appropriate, offer ways to help. For example, if Kia notices that Jonathan is upset because he didn't get a turn with the plastic dinosaur he wanted, she could offer one that is similar or offer to give it to him when she is finished.

Along with teaching the child an extensive vocabulary for expressing feelings, some children will need to learn to control their impulses so that they don't hurt others. Teach a child to recognize the physical signs that indicate their emotions are escalating. She might notice that her stomach feels funny, she has her fist clenched, or that her jaw has tightened (Hewitt and Heidemann, 2002). Once she learns her signals, teach her how to calm down. She can take deep breaths, count to five, or take a break from the activity. She will also need to learn to do something besides hit. Emphasize the options she has such as talking to a teacher, crossing her arms over her chest while she talks it out, telling the other child to stop, or moving away.

Once a child is learning to control her impulses, the early childhood practitioner can guide her through the step in problem solving. Teaching these skills to a child when she is not upset is important. Use puppets, stories with problems to solve, and role plays to teach the process before expecting a child to use the skills in the middle of a heated argument. Provide as much support as the child needs to work through the steps.

It takes many people well into adulthood to learn and routinely use problem-solving techniques for resolving conflicts. Practitioners could work with some children who are just beginning to learn the process and others who are veterans. Whatever skill level the child has, the practitioner needs to recognize what level of support the child needs and adapt her responses to it. When a child is unable to perform many of the problem-solving tasks independently, the adult will need to walk her through the steps. A child, who has more skills might only need the adult to offer support by standing nearby and acting as a resource if necessary.

> **Basic Steps in Problem Solving**
>
> 1. Identify the problem.
>
> 2. Calm down.
>
> 3. Think of solutions.
>
> 4. Try the best one.
>
> **Words to Guide the Process**
>
> 1. "I see you both are upset. Tell me about your argument."
>
> 2. "Take a deep breath and calm down."
>
> 3. "What could you do to work it out?"
>
> 4. "Which idea do you want to try?"
>
> Adapted from Deborah Hewitt, *So This Is Normal, Too.* Redleaf Press, St. Paul, MN. © 1995 www.redleafpress.org. ‡

Caring for Oneself

Working with children takes a lot of physical and emotional energy. Working with children who have emotional and behavioral challenges can require even more. People working with young children who feel

Ideas for Self Care

- Take a bubble bath.
- Engage in a hobby.
- Read a good book.
- Listen to your favorite music.
- Call a friend.
- Go to a movie.
- Work out.
- Take a walk, run, swim, or ride bike.
- Get a massage.
- Find a way to laugh.
- Develop a new interest outside of work. ✸

good about themselves are more likely to pass that feeling on to others. It is essential that practitioners care for themselves so they can better care for others. If a practitioner has not met her own physical, emotional, and social needs, she is less likely to interact, have the energy to meet challenges, and could lack the patience to cope.

Each person will find what is most important for him or her. It may be a single event done daily or a combination of things throughout the week. Self-care includes attention to physical health, proper nutrition, adequate sleep, and exercise. Finding time to relax, be with friends, and engage in recreational activities can help a person meet their own needs. Taking care of emotional needs enables practitioners to find the kindness and compassion required to support a child's emotional needs. For some, this might mean finding a confidant with whom to share concerns. For others, it might mean seeking professional counseling to gain self-awareness and heal past pains. Taking the necessary steps toward self-care provides practitioners with the fortitude and stamina needed for caring for children with challenging behaviors.

Summary

Some children have life experiences and neurological challenges that create greater emotional and behavioral needs. These children can be challenging to work with, yet they need even greater support and understanding from the people who care for them. The relationships that are built within the early childhood setting can set the stage for success. A child who has an adult who cares deeply about them and believes in their ability to succeed can overcome a great deal of adversity.

The nurturing practitioner strives to understand the child's background and influences on his behavior. They seek to guide the child's behavior in ways that build his feelings of worth and competence. The practitioner offers a setting that is developmentally appropriate with activities that a child is challenged by, yet can successfully complete. They model caring relationships and foster positive interactions between children. The community that is built is one in which each child knows he belongs.

The practitioner who is able to guide the behaviors of a child with emotional and behavioral challenges is secure in their abilities. This practitioner studies growth and development, critically reflects on performance, recognizes where improvements can be made, and continues education through classes, reading, and learning from others.

Every child deserves to have a practitioner with these skills and this level of commitment. A child who faces emotional and behavioral challenges will develop a healthy sense of self when she is invited into a secure relationship with a practitioner of this caliber.

KEY POINTS

1. Practitioners need to guard against labeling children who demonstrate challenging behaviors as "challenging" or "difficult."

2. Adults who live or work with young children take on many roles: detective, guide, role model, and nurturer.

3. There are many internal and external factors that influence a child's behavior. Early childhood practitioners can control some of the external factors such as: the environment they arrange for children, the schedule they create, and the activities and materials they provide. They also have control of their interactions with a child and the quality of the relationship they maintain. Many other factors are outside a practitioner's control.

4. The relationship between the very young child and those who care for her creates a blueprint for all relationships that follow. Children thrive when they are in trusting, loving, respectful relationships. These positive relationships help children feel safe, build self-esteem, and provide a basis for guiding a child's behavior.

5. A child's self-esteem is influenced by the messages received from caregivers concerning their characteristics and their behaviors. Provide specific information about what each child is doing well.

6. Practitioners may have heard messages as they were growing up that affected them positively or negatively. These phrases and the phrases they use with children can be examined. Practitioners can make choices about the messages they want children to hear and the phrases they will use. It is possible for adults to relearn how to express emotions and communicate feelings of anger.

7. Young children need adults to help them learn to identify and express their emotions as well as learn to meet their needs in acceptable ways. Practitioners can help children learn to recognize when they feel angry and provide options for expressing themselves.

8. People working with young children who feel good about themselves are more likely to pass that feeling on to others. Working with children takes emotional and physical energy. Taking care of children with challenging behaviors requires more energy. Practitioners can make certain to care for their own needs to prepare them to better meet the needs of others.

REFERENCES

Gartrell, D. (2004). *The Power of Guidance: Teaching Social-Emotional Skills in Early Childhood Classrooms.* Clifton Park, NY: Delmar Publishing.

Hewitt, D. & Heidemann, S. (2002). *The Optimistic Classroom: Creative Ways to Give Children Hope.* St. Paul: Redleaf Press.

Hyson, M. (2004). *The Emotional Development of Young Children: Building an Emotion-Centered Curriculum.* New York: Teachers College.

Kurcinka, M. (2006). *Raising Your Spirited Child* (Rev. ed.) New York: Harper Collins.

SUGGESTED READING

Heimes, M. (2009). "Teachers on Teaching: Building Positive Relationships." *Young Children, 64 (1),* 94–95.

Hewitt, D. (2011). *So This is Normal Too? Teachers and Parents Working Out Developmental Issues in Young Children.* St. Paul: Redleaf Press.

Katz, L., & McClellan, D. (1997). *Fostering Children's Social Competence: The Teacher's Role.* Washington, DC: NAEYC.

Keenan, M. "They Pushed My Buttons: Being Put Up Against Myself." *Young Children, 51,* 74–75.

Kuschner, A., Cranor, L., & Brekken, L. (Eds.) (1996). *Project EXCEP-TIONAL: A Guide for Training and Recruiting Child Care Providers to Serve Young Children with Disabilities.* Sacramento: California Department of Education.

Meece, D. & Soderman, A. (2010). "Positive Verbal Environments: Setting the Stage for Young Children's Social Development." *Young Children, (65)5,* 81-86.

Watson, M. (2003). "Attachment Theory and Challenging Behaviors: Reconstructing the Nature of Relationships." *Young Children, 58 (4),* 12–20.

Weinreb, M. (1997). "Be a Resiliency Mentor: You May be a Lifesaver for a High-risk Child." *Young Children, 52,* 14–20.

CHAPTER 2

Prevention:
It Is All About Environment

Cecelia Westby

Introduction

RE YOUNG children influenced by their environment? Yes. In fact, there is a direct connection between a young child's environment and the prevention of challenging behaviors. Early childhood practitioners can modify, adapt and change the young child's environment to promote optimal growth and development of all children (Deiner, 1999). Therefore, early childhood practitioners' decision-making should focus on the understanding that young children are clearly affected by their early childhood setting. Similar to adults, young children instantaneously determine if an environment feels good to them. According to Greenman (1998), the environment "conditions how we feel, think, and behave; it dramatically affects the quality of our lives. The environment either works for or against us as we conduct our lives." Rather than asking if young children are influenced, a better question could be, "How can we positively influence young children through their early childhood environment?" Each day of a young child's life is an opportunity to promote the child's growth and development toward becoming a healthy, contributing member of larger society. For many of today's young children, part of this development is taking place as a result of their experiences in an early childhood environment. First and foremost it is important to recognize that, as Greenman states, "the environment is always influencing us." It is the role of early childhood practitioners to use the environment to positively influence the children in early childhood settings.

The early childhood practitioner must continue to strive to create a high quality early childhood setting that recognizes the role of the environment in preventing challenging behavior. To begin, we must define what we mean by a "high quality" early childhood care and education environment. The National Association for the Education of Young Children (1998) provides a rationale for providing a high quality environment by stating that the physical environment affects the behavior and development of the people, both children and adults, who live and work in it. The quality of the physical space and materials provided affects the level of involvement of the children and the quality of interaction between adults and children. The amount, arrangement, and use of space, both indoors and outdoors, are to be evaluated.

A high quality early childhood environment is one in which children feel like they belong; it is an environment filled with child-sized tables, chairs, and equipment that help children move around safely and successfully help themselves. It is an environment where children have the opportunity to choose from a variety of materials and activities, and use the materials in a way to create what they wish. A high quality environment combines both activities of the child's choice and practitioner-directed activities. At all times, practitioners are observing to ensure the high quality early childhood setting is meeting the needs of the individual child and the group as a whole. With the knowledge of the kind of high quality environment we are striving to create, we can dissect the environment into seven key components. The components include:

▶ Developmentally Appropriate Practice
▶ Emotional Environment
▶ Materials and Activities
▶ Physical Environment
▶ Daily Routine
▶ Activities
▶ Transitions

Through careful consideration of each of these components, practitioners make decisions that impact the way a child feels in the early

childhood setting, and consequently influence his behavior. When decisions are based on how children develop and learn—physically, emotionally, socially and cognitively—it is possible for each child to develop to their fullest potential within a high quality early childhood care and education environment (Bredekamp and Copple, 1997). Most importantly, it is the role of early childhood practitioners to recognize that the environment has a direct impact on children's behavior and is a critical component of promoting pro-social behavior.

Key Components of the Environment and Preventing Challenging Behaviors

Developmentally Appropriate Practice
Developmentally Appropriate Practice (DAP) is the overarching philosophy upon which quality early childhood practice is based. DAP uses the environment as a necessary element to promote optimal growth and development in young children. Initiated by the National Association for the Education of Young Children (NAEYC), national standards of excellence named Developmentally Appropriate Practice in early childhood programs, were established. These national standards are

based on years of research in the field of early childhood. DAP provides early childhood educators with a process for making decisions about the well being and education of young children. The decision-making process includes gathering information about the individual child and the group of children before deciding what kind of environment and activities to provide. For example, an early childhood classroom might include a mixed-age classroom of three-, four-, and five-year-olds. This information will aid the early childhood practitioner in choosing activities at different developmental levels so each child can feel successful. The practitioner could choose several puzzles, some with only a few pieces and others with several pieces, to ensure each child can successfully complete a puzzle if he chooses. Therefore, the practitioner makes decisions based on at least three important kinds of information and knowledge: (a) what is known about child development and learning; (b) what is known about strengths, interests and needs in the group; (c) knowledge of social and cultural contexts in which children

live to ensure experiences are meaningful, relevant, and respectful (Bredekamp and Copple, 1997). An early childhood environment that reflects this information and knowledge will allow for success at different developmental stages (painting at the easel with the choice of how to paint and what to paint), opportunities to participate in activities that follow the children's interests (if children seem particularly interested in birds, the practitioner can add more bird-related activities to the original plan), and attention to a variety of social and cultural backgrounds (pictures and books throughout the room that illustrate children of all skin colors and a variety of families such as, single parent families, blended families, and extended families). The knowledge of DAP guides decision-making for the early childhood practitioner in regard to children and the role of environment and prevention of challenging behaviors. For more information regarding Developmentally Appropriate Practices, read *Developmentally Appropriate Practice in the Early Childhood Programs* (NAEYC, 1997).

Emotional Environment

An emotional environment is defined as one where young children develop emotional well-being and a feeling of safety, acceptance, and belonging. Through developing a secure emotional environment, children are less likely to strike out, test rules, or become frustrated. The following story illustrates the value of forethought in meeting the special needs of a preschool child. Consider the goals of the environment and the rationale for the choices that the teacher makes below regarding the environment. The goals for the environment are defined as ways in which an early childhood practitioner can change, adapt, or modify the environment to meet the needs of a particular young child or group of children—the "how." The rationale is the reason behind making changes in the environment—the "why." Below are some questions a practitioner might ask regarding possible adjustments to the environment:

What are the individual child's interests?

What materials and activities could be made available to support this child's interest?

What kinds of changes to the physical environment would contribute to the child's feeling of being safe?

How can the daily routine help the child to feel secure?

What combinations of practitioner-directed and child-directed activities are needed to meet this child's needs?

Julie is an early childhood practitioner of a group of twenty-three four- and five-year-olds in an early childhood care and education setting. Julie performs a variety of activities, both teacher and child-directed throughout the eight-hour day. Julie provides many open-ended activities for the children such as painting and reading and writing centers. Julie also provides a circle time where she sings with the children, reads aloud and talks about how they might spend their day together. Julie was recently informed that a new child, Susan, who is visually impaired, would be joining her classroom. Susan is four years old and participates in the Early Childhood Special Education (ECSE) classes in the local school district. Within the ECSE classes, Susan is paired with special education teachers who individualize classroom activities to meet her needs and promote her development. Her mother needed care for Susan after her preschool ECSE class each day and sought out Julie's classroom setting.

Immediately, Julie began to prepare for Susan's arrival. Her emphasis became the environment and the kinds of adaptations she needed to make to promote Susan's healthy development. A number of questions came to mind. How can I use the environment to prevent challenging behaviors, such as running in the classroom and possibly knocking Susan down? How can I create a safe environment for Susan? How can I help Susan feel she belongs here? How can I introduce Susan to this environment, and to the children? Based on her knowledge of DAP, Julie knew she needed to find out more about Susan as an individual; her needs, interests and strengths, her developmental level, and her family; and what was important and meaningful to her as a member of her family and culture. Julie began the decision-making process and corresponding changes to her environment:

▶ Julie collaborated with the ECSE staff to find out more about Susan's developmental level and age appropriate learning expectations. Did Susan have additional special needs to consider? Could Susan walk unassisted? What kinds of personal needs did Susan have? What concrete changes can be made to the environment by applying knowledge of Developmentally Appropriate Practice?

▶ Julie talked with Susan and her family members to find out her needs as an individual. What specific interests did Susan have? What do we need to know, as early childhood practitioners, about Susan's family and culture to help make classroom experiences meaningful to her?

▶ Julie met with her teaching assistants to share fears and hopes upon Susan's arrival. The teaching team also talked about sensitivity to Susan's experience in the new environment. What can we do as teachers to help Susan feel safe and comfortable in our preschool environment? How can we help develop positive rapport with Susan's mother and earn her trust? What is the ideal environment for Susan? How can we demonstrate respect through the environment for Susan's special needs?

These informed questions and the decision-making processes are both critical components of DAP and a developmentally appropriate environment. Through posing the questions, Julie has begun to identify the goals of the environment in preventing challenging behavior. For example, Braille was placed on labels and positioned at Susan's height for identification of learning centers. Braille was also added to the daily schedule and placed near the door for easy access. The act of placing Braille throughout the preschool classroom may prevent Susan from feeling frustrated in her new environment. The other children, also an important part of the environment, participated by being introduced to Braille and a walking stick. Children were encouraged initially to take Susan's hand to lead her to different learning centers. The children felt important helping Susan and developed a sense of empathy for Susan's experience, which was different from their own. The children's participation prevented the need for them to demonstrate challenging behavior by feeling left out or neglected upon Susan's arrival. Through being included in the changing of the environment, the children felt valued. Additionally, both Susan and her mother were invited to visit the classroom several times before Susan joined the preschool classroom. Susan's familiarity with her new environment and the teachers and children prevented additional adjustment problems such as feeling insecure. Susan began her preschool experience feeling welcomed and safe in her new early childhood setting.

The critical knowledge of Developmentally Appropriate Practice guides early childhood practitioners in sound decision-making and prevention of challenging behaviors. The environment, in Jim Greenman's words (1988), "is either a pleasing place to be or it isn't." And, according to Bunnett and Davis (1997), "We cannot ask children to give us their best if they do not feel safe, secure, and loved in the place where they work and play." Julie and her teaching assistants positively influenced the children's behavior through the environment and, therefore, influenced the impact on not only Susan, but also the other preschool children and teachers. The practitioners provided an environment in which the preschool children could "give them and each other their best." The developmentally appropriate decisions made in a child's environment (and on the child's behalf) have a lasting impact on the child's behavior and experience in the early childhood care and education setting.

Materials and Activities

The selection of materials and activities in an early childhood setting will have a direct impact on the behavior of children. Early childhood practitioners need to consider the choice of materials and activities that promote more peaceful behavior in the early childhood setting where children spend their day or a part of their day. According to Honig and Wittmer (1996), "arrangements of space and varieties of toys and learning materials affect whether children act aggressively or cooperate more peacefully." The selection process for creating a cooperative environment include choosing a variety of materials and activities for both small and large group play, selecting toys and materials with a broad range of developmental levels and providing easy access of toys and materials to the children.

Materials and Children's Interests. How do practitioners decide what kinds of materials to include in an environment to promote cooperation? Practitioners decide, in part, through identification of children's interests in a process called assessment. According to McAfee and Leong (1997), "Assessment is more than just the collection of information; it is collection with a purpose." For this discussion, the purpose of assessment is to promote an environment that encourages cooperation and prosocial behavior through material and activity selection. By watching children, early childhood practitioners can determine their individual and group interests, the kinds of activities that engage them and which activities they find meaningful.

There are many ways to assess an early childhood environment. On a daily basis, according to High Scope (1996), "teachers observe children to see what activities and materials they choose, how they work with the materials, and how they interact with peers and adults." Early childhood practitioners might want to use a checklist to record these daily observations. For example, an observation checklist could include questions similar to the following:

> *What do children actually do with the selected materials?*
> *Do children have the skills to use materials successfully?*
> *Do children use materials appropriately and creatively?*
> *Which types of materials seem to stimulate dramatic play?*
>   *Group play?*
> *Do different children play differently with the same materials?*
> *Which materials hold children's interest the longest?*
> *Are there enough materials to keep children meaningfully involved?*
> *Which areas are rarely used during work time?*
> *Which interest areas and materials are selected most often?*
> *How do children ask for help with materials from adults?*
>   *From peers?*
> *Which play experiences seem to foster cooperative play?*
>   *Solitary play?*
>
> Dodge and Colker, 1996

Early childhood practitioners committed to preventing challenging behaviors could record observations and, then, make corresponding changes to the environment. The assessment process might occur alone or as part of a collaboration with co-practitioners. An example of the assessment process and corresponding changes to the environment occurs in the following scenario, which takes places in a preschool classroom.

The classroom consists of seven learning centers that include the library, writing center, sensory table, art, science, fine motor, and construction. There are two preschool boys, named Martin and Jacob, who have a new-found interest in the Science Center. The boys continue to return, again and again, to the Science Center. The teacher has noted their interest. The Science Center includes a birdfeeder filled with birdseed, photographs of birds, and real bird nests. Martin and Jacob are fascinated with the birdfeeder and birdseed. They hold the birdfeeder up and examine the contents. After several attempts to get a better view, Martin and Jacob decide to turn the birdfeeder upside down and dump the birdfeed in the center of the room on the carpeting. In this way, they can touch, smell and view the birdseed more closely.

The teacher, Sam, has noted their interest through informal assessment. He made the following observations: The boys continued to return to the birdfeeders throughout the week. Through asking questions, Sam has learned that both Martin and Jacob are unfamiliar with birdfeeders and birdseed. Martin lives in an apartment, does not have a backyard and has never owned a birdfeeder. Jacob is a child who is learning English as a second language and has not had birdfeeders and birdseed as a part of his experience. Sam also observed that the boys had the need to touch and play with the birdseed to learn about it. He understood that young children learn through exploration and discovery of materials. Sam believed that their interest was important and he wanted to enhance it—to promote their individual learning.

The following week, Sam changed the environment to reflect Martin and Jacob's interest. He filled the Sensory Table with birdseed, birdfeeders and scoops. This environmental change prevented the boys from using the carpeting as a play area and contained their play within a defined boundary—the Sensory Table. Sam also provided scoops and birdfeeders so the boys could fill, empty, and re-fill the birdfeeders as often as they liked. He then enhanced the Science Center by bringing in several different examples of various birdseeds, labeled and sealed in transparent bags. He named the bags "looking bags" and introduced the them to the children. Sam encouraged the children to look and learn at the Science Center. However, he told them if they wanted to feel and play with the birdseed, they needed to visit the Sensory Table.

The process of assessment helped Sam understand his children's individual needs. He then made environmental changes to meet the identified needs. In turn, the children's behavior was redirected from dumping the birdseed on the floor to playing with the birdseed within a defined area, the Sensory Table. Additional samples of birdseed were offered, allowing more children to experience the birdseed at different learning centers and in different ways. This type of careful consideration of child observations guides early childhood practitioners in choosing materials and activities that promote cooperation among the young children in their care.

Broad Developmental Range. Young children enjoy pretending, making messes, solving problems, and creating things—this is the work of children! Open-ended activities provide children with many opportunities to explore, discover and grow, and specifically work well with children who have special needs. Naturally, they also lend themselves to a broad range of developmental abilities as the result of having no "right answer." Open-ended activities are defined as "activities that have no correct outcome and do not have an arbitrary stopping point" (Greenman, 1988). Open-ended activities may also be described as "activities to children that involve them as active learners who act on objects and observe the results of their actions" (Althouse, 1988). An activity that is open-ended allows for children with different abilities to be successful. For example, all children may use the Sensory Table filled with water, buckets and scoops. Children with special needs may be successful accomplishing the tasks of scooping and pouring water even if less accurate when carrying out this process. Most importantly, the child with special needs can participate in the Sensory Table activity and feel good about it! Along with the activity is the opportunity for the practitioner to ask open-ended questions such as, How can you get the water into the bucket? How does the water feel on your hands? and Are there other ways you can get the water into the bucket? Practitioners may ask open-ended questions which both encourage and support the efforts of the children with special needs. According to *Art for the Fun of It* (Jenkins, 1993), the following are suggested materials and activities that lend themselves to open-ended activities.

▶ Pasting and assembling
▶ Tearing, cutting, and folding
▶ Drawing and rubbing
▶ Painting
▶ Modeling and carving
▶ Constructing

Other open-ended activity suggestions include: using a variety of music and movement activities throughout the day, encouraging children to use their imagination through storytelling, and promoting dramatic play (Dodge, Koralek & Pizzolongo, 1991).

Early childhood practitioners need to find ample opportunities to provide open-ended activities throughout the day. Also, when children cannot successfully participate in the activities or materials provided, they will challenge the practitioner. Through providing open-ended materials, early childhood practitioners encourage success for all children, regardless of developmental range.

Accessibility. Another way the environment plays a part in preventing challenging behavior is through the accessibility of all activities and materials. It is critical to "set up the environment so children can easily select, replace, and care for materials and equipment" (Dodge, Koralek and Pizzolongo, 1991). An environment that is child-friendly includes a space for the child's coat and personal belongings, low shelves that include pictures showing where materials belong, tables and chairs which fit the size of the child, clear traffic patterns from one area of the room to another, and areas that are sectioned off, possibly by shelves, to enclose the activity to prevent disruptions. Self-selection of materials and activities promotes children's sense of self-esteem. Children who help themselves and direct their own play will feel, "I can do it!" When children feel good about themselves and their accomplishments, they do not need to seek attention through mistaken behavior (Gartrell, 1998). The role of early childhood practitioners is to create an environment where access to materials and activities is thought out ahead of time with the child's present developmental level and interests in mind to ensure their success.

Physical Environment

The physical environment, or the way the space is arranged, has an important impact on children's behavior as well. In fact, "classroom layout affects children's emotional security" (Honig and Wittmer, 1996). Maria Montessori, physician and pioneer in studying children's intellectual development, believed in creating a "prepared environment" because children's responses to their environment can have important effects on their intellectual, social, and spiritual development (Katz and McClellan, 1997). There is also a strong belief by early childhood practitioners in the Reggio Emilio schools that, "the environment is one of the teachers" (Katz and McClellan, 1997). Even subtle changes in the physical environment can have an impact on children's behavior. A good example is child-sized chairs in an early childhood setting. Now commonplace, the idea to design and manufacture little chairs, originally came from Maria Montessori. She wanted to provide children the liberty to come and go as they needed, to carry out their play (Hunt, 1977).

The physical environment could be defined as the area where children spend their time, both indoors and outdoors, the arrangement of the space, and how the space is cared for. A good place to begin is to adopt an open attitude and recognize that early childhood practitioners are learning too! Practitioners are learning to prepare the best kind of environment for the particular group of young children. By studying what the children can do, both children who are typically developing and children with special needs, the physical space can be arranged. It may take subtle adjustments to the space to accommodate some special needs, such as the creation of wider corridors for a wheel-

Problem Behavior	Possible Causes	How to Change the Environment
● Wandering around; unable to choose activities	● Room too cluttered; choices not clear; not enough to do	● Get rid of clutter. Simplify the layout of the room and materials. Add more activity choices. Offer relevant activity choices.
● Materials used roughly; children resist cleaning up	● Materials on shelves are messy; no order to display of materials	● Make a place for everything. Use picture labels to show where things go.
● Easily distracted; trouble staying with a task	● Areas are undefined and open; children can see everything going on in the room	● Use shelves to define areas so children are not distracted by other activities.

chair, more room for a child to lie down as she plays, flooring that is not slippery nor shaggy, higher or lower workspaces and special chairs (Greenman, 1988). Other physical space considerations may include: "providing a quiet space, for some children. Other children might need additional space cues, such as tape on the floor or a special rug during circle time" (Dodge and Colker, 1996).

Physical space layout can be determined by walking through the classroom setting or by drawing a simple diagram. For example, most children will break into a run if there is a long, narrow passageway ahead of them. The same is true for a classroom with open stretches of space. It is worthwhile to study the room floor plan from a child's viewpoint while walking through the classroom space. The practitioner will easily identify where to place learning centers and how to arrange equipment to discourage some behaviors. For other suggestions by Dodge and Colker (1996), see sidebar on this page.

Part of children's learning process is to help them make connections between things. Early childhood practitioners assist children in making and reinforcing learning connections through the physical environment, as well. In others words, by supporting their natural curiosity practitioners decrease boredom and associated negative behaviors. According to Gareau and Kennedy (1991):

> One way in which children grow toward logical thinking is by repeatedly experiencing connections between things. In organizing classroom space, we should attempt to position learning materials close to others with related learning objectives. Children's curiosity will then be a positive feature, since they can add what attracts their attention to their present activity.
>
> For example, practitioners may choose to place a fine motor activity such as the writing center, close to the library center. By grouping the reading and writing centers, practitioners will reinforce children's learning about how writing and reading are interconnected. In this way, early childhood practitioners hope to engage and maintain their interest and, therefore, reduce and prevent problematic behaviors.

Daily Routine

A daily routine is another critical component of a successful early childhood setting. This is supported by Bunnett and Davis (1997) who state, "We have learned that even with a well-designed space, if our daily schedule is too rigid or controlling, all the messages we want to convey are compromised." With that in mind, early childhood practitioners must design the daily schedule to allow for alternating periods of active and quiet time, adequate nutrition, and naptime (for younger children). Teachers allocate extended periods of time (at least one hour) for children to engage in play and projects. Children have ample time to explore and learn about the environment, investigate what sparks their curiosity, and experiment with cause-and-effect relationships (Bredekamp and Copple, 1997).

Although a set schedule is important, the flexibility of the schedule must be emphasized. For children with special needs, the practitioner can create an activity board with activity choices. Attaching a strip of Velcro hook fasteners to the center makes the activity board. Next, the practitioner could color or photocopy pictures of activities that are available to the child in the early childhood setting. Then, she can attach Velcro loop fasteners to the back of each piece with a picture of the activity on it. The child could select the piece that indicates his next choice of activity and place it on the board. This method allows the child flexibility in both the choice of activity and the order in which he participates in each activity. Some activities may be shorter or longer, depending upon the day and the chosen activity. In addition, children's maturity levels and their ability to sit vary by age and developmental level. In other words, a young three-year-old may sit for only a few minutes, whereas when he is closer to four, he may be capable of sitting for an entire story or song. This is based on watching the children in the program and noting their attention and interest levels on any particular day (Walmsley, Camp, and Walmsley, 1992). An optimum feeling to which early childhood practitioners may aspire is one where children "feel alert yet totally relaxed and in control of their choices" (Katz and McClellan, 1997). There is enough of a pre-planned daily schedule for the children to feel secure but enough flexibility to respect the individual child's needs and interests. This describes an optimal learning environment for young children to grow.

Activities

There is much support for early childhood programs with a balance of practitioner-directed and child-centered activity. Practitioner di-

rected activities might also be called formal activities such as circle time, singing, finger plays, and reading aloud where the practitioner takes the lead. Conversely, there are informal activities that consist of child-centered choice time, when each child can choose how, when, and where they spend that time. Research supports that "early childhood programs that are excessively teacher-directed and academic in orientation, yield undesirable effects" (Katz and McClellan, 1997). The "undesirable effects" are behaviors that practitioners try to prevent—such as aggression—through a well-balanced early childhood program.

The opportunity for a child to make choices is an important self-esteem builder. "If we want to raise children to be responsible decision-makers and social problem-solvers, we need to give them the message, early in the preschool years, that they are capable of making decisions, solving problems, and taking responsibility" (Graves, 1996). For comparison, imagine if a practitioner were in a setting where choices could not be made, ideas were not valued, and solutions were met with an unaccepting attitude—the practitioner could feel powerless and hold a lesser self-image. On the other hand, when children and adults, feel that their ideas, interests, and solutions are met with interest and encouragement, the individual's sense of self-esteem is strengthened and allowed to flourish. According to Graves (1999), "If we want (children) to develop confidence in their abilities, we need to listen to, accept, and allow them to follow through on their ideas." This is the premise for child-centered activities.

Adult-directed activities must be engaging, developmentally appropriate in length, and support children's need to move, relax their bodies, and promote listening skills. Early childhood practitioners who observe their children and plan activities accordingly will have more success in providing engaging activities that are meaningful to the children, both individually and as a group. Another important component of a successful adult-directed activity is movement. Children who are active tend to be more alert and learn more (Dennison and Dennison, 1994). Finger plays and activities that encourage the children to stand and move around will benefit their learning during adult-directed times. In addition to feeling alert, children should feel relaxed in their early childhood educational setting. When children feel relaxed, they are more receptive to learning (Katz and McClellan, 1997). And finally, a child who is engaged in a story or activity will naturally listen for a longer period of time. However, it is important to note that young children are not developmentally able to sit for long periods of time. A mix of active and quiet times within the adult-directed activities will help to prevent boredom or mistaken behavior. Author Deiner (1999) recommends the goals and activities listed below for children with diverse abilities.

Practitioners need time and opportunity to make adjustments to the schedule and, then, observe the children's reactions to the changes. After a period of observation, the practitioner should ask, What is working with the daily schedule? What could be improved upon? They should continue this three-step process: change, observe, and reflect. Practitioners might want to carry out the three-step process periodically throughout the year or as other changes, such as child group dynamics, demand it. Most importantly, practitioners must keep their intention—using the environment to prevent aggressive behaviors—at the forefront of the decision-making in regard to the activities.

Transitions

Waiting can be difficult for young children because they focus on the here and now and are "unable to wait very long, regardless of the promised outcome" (Bredekamp and Copple, 1997). An acceptance of this

Goal	Practitioner-directed Activity
To increase child's body awareness	Read a story while child relaxes their body. Ask child to move her body in response to directions.
To improve child's fine motor skills	Photograph child enjoying class activity. Cut photograph into puzzle pieces. Collect buttons, two of a kind, and an egg carton. Child will sort objects by touch.
To help child express feelings	Discuss broad range of feelings. Ask child to share a feeling with a classmate. Teach the children tongue twisters and ask them to repeat it fast. Encourage children to talk about how they feel after saying a difficult tongue twister fast.

developmental truth goes a long way in using the environment to have a direct impact on young children's behavior. Children, both those who are developing typically and those with special needs, must feel secure in their environment. This feeling of security in children contributes to creating an environment that is both peaceful and cooperative. Security is established, in part, when children know what comes next in their daily routine.

Some simple adaptations to the routine will assist young children in making successful transitions. For example, early childhood practitioners must prepare children in advance for changes during the day by stating, "We will be cleaning up our space in five minutes." Although young children may not be able to logically determine five minutes, it gives them time to start thinking about the clean up process. When children are surprised with instant changes, they may respond unfavorably. This is to be expected as Maria Montessori stated, "play is child's work." Again, practitioners can put themselves in the child's "shoes." As an adult, when practitioners are deeply engaged in a work project, how would it feel to be abruptly interrupted and to leave an activity right now? The initial reaction may be anger, disappointment, frustration, or an unsettled feeling attributed to the need to complete an activity. The same is true for children. When they are deeply engrossed in play, their feelings need to be respected so they too can end one activity and prepare for the next.

Summary

The early childhood environment has an impact on children's behavior. In the role of early childhood practitioners, the decisions made in regard to the environment will determine whether the classrooms are filled with children who exhibit aggressive behaviors or a place where children exhibit peaceful, cooperative behavior. Through careful choices within the environment, practitioners support children's need to feel safe, loved, and valued. This is the foundation upon which using the environment to prevent and decrease challenging behaviors rests. When practitioners study the seven essential components of a successful environment, the knowledge of the role the environment plays as "one of the teachers" will contribute to a successful classroom environment. The practitioner can use the seven key points of a child's

environment below to assist in making choices that prevent challenging behaviors from young children. The seven key points are:

► Developmentally appropriate practice
► Emotional environment
► Materials and activities
► Physical environment
► Daily routine
► Activities
► Transitions

KEY POINTS

1. The importance of the impact of environment on behaviors is one
of the underlying philosophies of Developmentally Appropriate Practice (DAP). The philosophy of DAP insists that practitioners come to
know each child as an individual—their strengths, needs and interests,
developmental level, and their part as a member of their family and a
specific culture.

2. When children enter a space, they get a feeling about it; they
might feel insecure or secure or they might feel welcome or unwel-
come. Early childhood practitioners need to prepare the space with a
child's perspective in mind—the need to feel safe, loved, and valued—
and create a safe, inviting environment. Areas must include space for
active times and quiet times. Through identification of problematic areas, early childhood educators can change the environment and have
an impact on children's behavior.

3. Through careful consideration, materials and activities are chosen following the observation of individual and group interests. The
process of observation will ensure children's interests are honored and
opportunities for both small and large group play are available. Additionally, early childhood practitioners will provide open-ended materials and activities. The open-ended activities will promote success and
increased feelings of self-esteem for children with a broad range of developmental levels.

4. Arranging the environment requires attention and care to indoor
and outdoor spaces.

5. Children will gain security through a schedule that is both set and flexible. The "set" schedule assures children of the daily order of events thereby providing security. The "flexibility" of the daily schedule allows for the early childhood practitioner to meet the individual and group needs of children. Some activities require more time while others will not take as long as planned.

6. Through a balance of both practitioner-directed and child-centered activity, children will flourish developmentally. The early childhood practitioner must engage children and provide for opportunities for movement, relaxation, and listening. The length of the time that children are asked to sit is important; young children might sit for short periods of time, followed by the opportunity to move their bodies. Children asked to sit for long periods of time without movement could become disruptive. Young children must also have the opportunity to choose how to use part of their time. Children need ample time—about one hour per day—in child-centered activity where they can select and direct their own play. A combination of both practitioner-directed and child-centered activity promotes the healthy development of children.

7. Children feel secure when they know their daily schedule. The elimination of surprises or abrupt departures from one activity to the next will decrease problems associated with not enough time to end an activity before beginning another. Early childhood practitioners need to provide warnings before a change in activity. A warning needs to be followed by enough time for the children to complete their current activity.

REFERENCES

Althouse, R. (1988). *Investigating Science with Young Children*. NY: Teachers College Press.

Berk, L. (2000). *Child Development*. (2nd ed.). Needham Heights, MA: Allyn & Bacon.

Bredekamp, S. & Copple, C. (1997). *Developmentally Appropriate Practice in Early Childhood Programs*. Washington, DC: NAEYC.

Bunnett, R. & Davis, N. (1997). *Getting to the Heart of the Matter. Child Care Information Exchange, 114*, 42–44.

Deiner, P. (1999). *Resources for Educating Children with Diverse Abilities*. Sea Harbor Drive, OR: Harcourt, Brace and Company.

Dennison, P. & Dennison, D. (1994). *Brain Gym: Teacher's Manual*. Ventura, CA: Edu-Kinesthetics.

Dodge, D., Colker, L., and Heroman, C. (1996). *The Creative Curriculum For Preschool* (4th ed.). Washington, DC: Teaching Strategies.

Dodge, D., Koralek, D. and Pizzolongo, P. (1991). *Caring for Preschool Children*. Washington, DC: Teaching Strategies.

Elkind, D. (1981). *The Hurried Child*. Reading, MA: Addison-Wesley Publishing Company.

Fisher, B. (1998). *Joyful Learning in Kindergarten*. Portsmouth, NH: Heineman.

Gareau, M. & Kennedy, C. (1991). "Structure Time & Space to Promote Pursuit of Learning in the Primary Grades," *Young Children*. *46*, 46–51.

Gartrell, D. (1998). *A Guidance Approach for the Encouraging Classroom*. Albany, NY: Delmar Publishers.

Graves, M. (1996). *Planning Around Children's Interests*. Ypsilanti, MI: High/Scope Educational Research Foundation.

Greenman, J. (1988). *Caring Spaces, Learning Places: Children's Environments that Work*. Redmond, WA: Exchange Press Inc.

Honig, A. & Wittmer, D. (1996). "Helping Children Become More Pro-Social: Ideas for Classrooms, Families, Schools and Communities," *Young Children, 51*, 62–70.

Jenkins, P. (1993). *Art For the Fun of It*. NY: Prentice Hall Press.

Katz, L. & McClellan, D. (1997). *Fostering Children's Competence: The Teacher's Role*.

McAfee, O. & Leong, D. (1997). *Assessing and Guiding Young Children's Development and Learning*. Needham Heights, MA: Allyn & Bacon.

Hunt, J. McV. (1977). *Montessori, Maria: The Montessori Method*. NY: Schocken Books.

NAEYC. (1998). *Accreditation Criteria & Procedures of the National Association for the Education of Young Children*. Washington, DC: NAEYC.

Walmsley, B., Camp, A., and Walmsley, S. (1992). *Teaching Kindergarten: A Developmentally Appropriate Approach*. Portsmouth, NH: Heineman.

CHAPTER 3

Inside the Child: Social and Emotional Development

Dr. Lynn Gehrke

Introduction

ARLY childhood practitioners play an important role in the academic development of young children. School readiness, kindergarten readiness and standardized testing are three of the many current issues that provide the push toward a greater emphasis on academic development in the early years. It's not often, in this conversation, that the connection between academic development and social/ emotional development is made. The truth is, development in the emotional and cognitive domains is connected at all levels—each is necessary for the other. A child's ability to regulate her strong emotions, or find words to express them, rests on her ability to think through her choices and options. Caring, responsive, consistent attention to infants by early childhood practitioners prompts the development of the infants' trust in people, their environment, and their ability to have their needs met. When practitioners teach toddlers new words to use when conflicts arise over a toy, they help toddlers make deposits in their "word banks" for future use. Finally by teaching preschoolers to stop, take a deep breath, and try again, the practitioner provides new skills necessary for future self-control. These strategies involve both cognitive and social/emotional development.

Children typically move through stages of gaining social and emotional competence at different rates of time. But sometimes adults believe that children automatically know how to act in social situations. The truth is, in the early years, children do not yet have either the intellectual development or emotional resources to make a mature response to a difficult social situation or a strong emotional feeling. If early childhood practitioners can think of children's mistakes in social situations like this, they are better able to see them as worthwhile, typically developing, and ready to learn more suitable ways to act. This chapter presents the typical stages of social/emotional development and how early childhood practitioners can help children develop competence in this area.

Connection Between Emotional Development and Social Learning

The most important form of social/emotional development that takes place in infancy is attachment. Attachment is the positive emotional bond that develops between a child and an important adult. The nature of a child's attachment during infancy has an impact on how she relates to others throughout the rest of her life. With consistent care, human touch, and responsive attention, a baby not only develops a healthy attachment to her parents and/or early childhood practitioners; she learns to trust others and her environment.

With this trust solidly developed, a child's sense of self—her autonomy—begins to take shape and continues throughout early childhood. A child with a healthy sense of self demonstrates an interest in new things, a desire to discover on her own, an ability to leave the side of a trusted adult to explore, and a strong interest in social situations. All these abilities connect healthy emotional development to such social learning as self-regulation, ability to join an ongoing playgroup, and the skills to work through conflict or cooperation.

Typically by age three, early childhood practitioners

expect young children to learn these social traits. However, if practitioners expect too much or too little from young children, they might demonstrate their frustration through challenging behaviors. With healthy emotional development such as a strong sense of attachment to caring adults and a developing sense of self, children can and do accomplish the social learning necessary for successful academic learning and for life if the skills are modeled carefully by early childhood practitioners.

Sequence of Emotional Development

Dr. Bruce Perry, M.D., Ph.D., an internationally recognized authority on brain development and children in crisis, has labeled the sequence of emotional development for children as *Six Core Strengths* (2002). The essence of the sequential stages will seem familiar to the early childhood practitioner but some of the labels may be new. A child must develop the following emotional and social skills in order—each child will move through at her own rate. These skills are: attachment, self-regulation, affiliation, awareness, tolerance, and respect. As familiar as these seem, the following sections will explain and expand on each stage.

Attachment
This stage is the most important. Attachment is a special form of a bond! It is:

- ▶ Positive.
- ▶ Predictable.
- ▶ The first relationship with a special person.
- ▶ Soothing, comfortable, and pleasurable.
- ▶ Created by what both the child and adult bring to the relationship.
- ▶ Created by optimal caregiving in the first year of life.
- ▶ Responsible for the creation of an emotional template in the brain by which all incoming relationships are judged.

Development of the other stages is difficult without healthy attachment. Without it, children do not respond to the practitioner's encouragement or teaching strategies. These children find no pleasure in engaging with others and no discomfort in displeasing others. With-

Six Key Strengths that Children Must Develop

1. **Attachment**—the capacity to form and maintain relationships is at the foundation of the creation of a healthy child.

2. **Self-Regulation**—the ability to read and respond to internal states appropriately. If children are unable to recognize what's going on inside them, getting along with others and regulating behavior is difficult.

3. **Affiliation**—the ability to join with others and contribute to a group is a very important skill. If children haven't developed self-regulation, they will have difficulty with affiliation.

4. **Awareness**—the capacity to recognize the needs, interests, strengths, and value in others. Young children see people in simple groups, which interferes with seeing people as they really are. Children must be with people who are different. Children must have a chance to be with elderly and children of other ages, too.

5. **Tolerance**—a child's capacity to understand and accept how others are different from themselves.

6. **Respect**—the capacity to value the variety of gifts and capacities of others and in yourself. This concept is the most difficult. If children can't accept their own shortcomings, self-respect is difficult, which causes them to focus on the shortcomings of others in a negative way. When we raise our children with "don't do this, don't do that," the brain spends so much more time focusing on shortcomings rather than strengths. It is important to help children develop in a positive way.

More on these strengths can be found at
http://www.lfcc.on.ca/Perry_Six_Core_Strengths.pdf

out attachment, children behave impulsively without regret. Healthy development of attachment requires structure, predictability, nurturing, and the stimulations of all five senses during the first years of life.

Factors Involved in the Development of Attachment. There are several factors necessary to ensure healthy attachment. The sharing of emotional expression strengthens the adult-child bond. Babies vocalize and respond to a joyful face. A practitioner in  the infant room who is familiar to the babies creates a secure base for the children. When this practitioner engages in playful talk, laughter, and responsive reaction, the child begins developing a healthy attachment. Infants detect the emotions of others within the first months of life and match the feeling tone of their caregiver. Once the child begins to understand the meanings related to emotional expression, she begins to look for information through the emotions of the trusted practitioner and use it to guide her own behavior. It is important that the early childhood practitioner understands this emotional give-and-take because the involvement is crucial to fostering healthy attachment.

A child's innate temperament—her way of reacting to the world, her activity level, and her level of self-regulation—can affect her emotional expressions, thereby affecting the development of healthy attachment. The three defined types of temperament are the easy child, the spirited child, and the slow-to-warm-up child. A child with an easy temperament establishes predictable routines early in infancy and is usually cheerful and adaptable. A child with a spirited temperament has unpredictable daily routines and tends to react negatively and intensely. A child who is slow-to-warm-up might need more time to get acclimated each day, especially if there are new activities introduced. As might be assumed here, the practitioner's ability to interact with a child who has a spirited temperament is extremely different from the interaction with a child who has an easy temperament. Practitioners must accept and respond to each child's unique temperament by creating environments that encourage children's strengths and foster their development. The sensitive caregiving described here demands that the adult attends to the needs and temperament of each child. What is sensitive caregiving? It is attending to children's needs, creating connectedness with others, helping them acquire new skills, providing positive encouragement, ensuring that their daily routines are predictable, helping them enjoy their environment, learning more about their family, developing a positive relationship with their parents, and doing it all with consistency and loving responsiveness. The early childhood practitioner who practices these strategies with young children and who creates an emotionally secure environment goes a long way to promoting the development of healthy attachment. This healthy attachment creates a sense of trust for the infant and is the basis for the development of self-regulatory skills necessary for behavior control.

Self-Regulation

To be able to get along in life and participate in groups of other children and adults, children must be able to read and respond to their own internal states appropriately. In fact, regulating one's internal feelings and cognitive development are directly tied together. Brain function creates the basis and context for the self-talk and self-soothing strategies children learn when they experience a trusting and caring relationship early in life. These self-regulatory skills are the foundation of the healthy emotional development necessary for the development of life-long social skills. Children who are unable to recognize what is going on inside them have a slower social development that could create problems for them when they want to interact with others. As a result, providing the time necessary and helping children develop these skills is the important work of early childhood professionals.

Young children learn to ask for water when they are thirsty, run to a caring adult when something frightens them, and find a place to curl up when they are sleepy. It is these built-in responses to bodily needs that children learn to seek because of the warm, consistent, responsive care they have received. When practitioners repeatedly provide for the needs of young children, they help children strengthen their ability to regulate feelings. Actually, by consistently responding to a child's needs, a practitioner can teach a child to wait for a reply after asking for her needs to be met rather than scream, cry, or shout. This important social/emotional skill can be thought of as helping children put a pause between an impulse and an action.

This development allows the child to feel calm and act more "mature" (the cognitive connection) when frustrations arise from the emotional, social, and cognitive challenges of development. With the ability to put a pause between impulse and action, the child can take time to think and plan, and, usually, come up with an appropriate response to the current challenge. This pause ability does not happen automatically. The practitioner's role in this skill development is to teach children patience, how to wait, and how to calm themselves.

Factors Involved in the Development of Self-Regulation. When the practitioner in the infant/toddler room provides consistent responses to the child's impulses, she provides the emotional wiring necessary for self-regulation. Many factors are involved in this consistent response such as appropriate scheduling and activities, programming, and practices that meet each child's individual needs, knowledge of typical development in early childhood, knowledge of the cause of behaviors and the effective response, and partnership with parents.

In addition to these factors, practitioners actually teach the words necessary for creating the pause between the impulse and action. For example:

> A three-year-old in your group really wants to play with his favorite truck, but someone else has it. In fact, because you know it is a favorite, you have a second one just like it for times like this. But, the second one is in use, too. Your knowledge of this child tells you that he may get frustrated quickly when he realizes neither truck is available (typical emotional reaction for a child his age). To increase his self-regulatory skills—the ability to be frustrated internally, calm down, and ask for help—you move closer to him as he walks toward the block center where the trucks are. When he realizes both trucks are "busy," you are there to provide emotional support and teach him the words that he needs to talk to himself and ask for help.
>
> You observe him as he notices that other children are using the trucks. You watch for signs of frustration. To create self-regulatory skills you want to put the pause between the impulse and action. He starts to make a growling noise, signaling to you that his frustration level is building. You move closer and say, "Aaron, I notice you are making a growling noise, are you okay?" He shrugs away from you and you try again, "Aaron, you are

making a growling noise and it makes me think you want something." He says, "Uh-huh. I want my truck." You reply, "Aaron, oh, you want the truck you like to play with here at school, the red one, right?" He says, "Uh-huh, but they got my trucks." "Aaron, you are right, Sherrie has one truck and Jared has the other." He restates his desire, "I want my truck." You persist saying, "Aaron I know you are really frustrated, because your voice is getting loud and your face looks like this. Let's ask what they are doing and when they will be done."

You go on to help Aaron ask Sherrie and Jared what they are playing. You are very clear with your words and give Aaron words to practice using. You stay physically close to Aaron, holding his hand, rubbing his back, smiling and providing reassurance to offset his stress. You finally suggest, "Aaron, ask Sherrie if you can play with the truck when she's done. Say it like this, 'Sherrie, may I have the truck when you are done?'" You are prepared to say the words for him if he can't. You wait for Sherrie's response and continue to negotiate, teaching Aaron new words and helping him put the pause between his impulse and action. After Aaron and Sherrie make their deal, you offer to play with Sherrie, Aaron, and Jared. You ask what they are doing, and you and Aaron join the ongoing playgroup. Occasionally, you remind Aaron that he is waiting for the truck very patiently. When Sherrie is done and gives Aaron the truck, you teach him to thank Sherrie and thank her, too, for remembering that he was waiting. You remind Aaron that he really wanted the truck, but he used words to say what he wanted, he waited for his turn, and he thanked Sherrie when she gave it to him.

This kind of self-regulation teaching provides the emotional support that young children need as they continue their journey toward emotional development and social learning. Some children have trouble with self-regulation despite the teaching strategies and support techniques of the early childhood practitioner. The behaviors that result can disrupt an early childhood setting. These children are often overly sensitive to transitions and tend to overreact to minor changes in the setting. They need structure and predictability from practitioners who model self-control in their words and actions when they are frustrated themselves.

Affiliation

Affiliation is the ability to work, and play with others and be able to add value to the group—all of which are important social and emotional skills in the preschool years. If a child has a problem with self-regulation, affiliation is difficult. Interacting with others in a playgroup, an early childhood setting, or during social play (all skills related to affiliation) requires an ability to delay gratification, express strong emotions or feelings, and calm frustrations. Without it, classroom turmoil can develop and prevent play from creating learning.

Practitioners must not underestimate the role of play in the preschool years. Many writers have documented its role in cognitive development. The practitioner's role in play as tutor, facilitator, and observer is critical, if learning is to take place. However, it is very important for the practitioner to understand that when children play together, they begin to learn social rules. Watch children play. It is easy to notice the advanced social play skills of the children who have siblings at home or have been involved in early childhood settings or play groups. They participate in the give-and-take of developing the rules of their play, actually mimicking the social rules all people must learn to get along in life.

The response of the adults to children's attempts at affiliation can make a difference in their ability to develop this emotional and social skill. That response is even more critical if the child has a spirited or slow-to-warm-up temperament because it may take these children longer to fine tune their affiliation skills. The children with spirited temperaments may run headlong into an ongoing playgroup without stopping to observe or ask for an invitation. Children with slow-to-warm-up temperaments need gentle encouragements to even approach the group. Practitioners can help by teaching children the actual words they need to communicate their desire to join others in play. Children with both temperaments benefit when their small success toward affiliation is recognized and encouraged.

Factors Involved in the Development of Affiliation. The ability to participate with others in play does not happen overnight. As children learn the social skills related to play, they first must watch what the other children are doing. The skilled practitioner watches for children who need help with this first skill of affiliation. As children move from play that is more solitary to the type that is more social, the practitioners' responsiveness and attention to their play will provide support and guidance toward the development of affiliation skills. As mentioned earlier, children with spirited or slow-to-warm-up temperaments may

take longer to develop affiliation skills such as, entering an ongoing playgroup, participation in social play themes, or turn taking. Even when their self-regulation skills have begun to emerge and they practice them without prompts from adults, these children need a child-directed setting that encourages play and discovery, where practitioners provide extra attention, direction, and gentle instruction to learn the social skills necessary for affiliation. The following play scenario demonstrates this.

Helping children like Cedric join a group and feel successful in doing so is important. Others often exclude children who act impulsively or shyly. This exclusion can become a pattern that reinforces the impulsive or shy behavior. The practitioner must be prepared to help children join playgroups within the class and foster an atmosphere of acceptance, safety, and unconditional respect for all. If not, the excluded children become targets for similar isolation and future low self-esteem. Without intervention by the practitioner, children may turn the inward pain of exclusion to outward behaviors that could be aggressive or violent. At the very least, a child who is excluded due to her inability to be a positive member of a group will affiliate with other chil-

MATTIE, Erin, and James are immersed in play in the classroom flower shop. James is the shopper, Mattie is the cashier, and Erin is the florist. All have matched their actions to their individual roles and have discussed how they are going to proceed. James has just walked up to the store and Erin has paper and pencil, ready to take his order. You notice that Cedric has approached Mattie with his eyes on the cash register. You know he likes to play with the register and he typically resists waiting his turn. To provide play assistance and tutoring for Cedric and the group he is approaching, you move close to Cedric and say, "Hi Cedric, looks like you are interested in playing flower shop with Mattie, Erin and James. Is that right?" Cedric nods, "Uh-huh, I want to do the register." As he speaks, he moves right toward Mattie's space. You answer, "Oh, you want to be a flower shop cashier. Ask Mattie what she's doing." If Cedric needs the words for this question, provide them for him. Mattie answers, "I'm the cashier. You can work in the flower shop with Erin. Here's an apron for you." Cedric reaches for the cash register and you say, "Cedric, did you hear Mattie? She is the cashier right now. Right Mattie?" "Right," Mattie answers. You offer Cedric a choice. "Cedric, Erin needs help filling orders. Would you like to work with her while you wait your turn to be cashier, or would you like to be a customer with James?" Cedric looks at James who has a wallet with pretend money and a calculator in his wallet to figure the prices. You know there is an extra wallet with the same equipment and offer it to Cedric with the choice. Cedric says, "James, want to shop together?" James says, "Let's buy some flowers and take them to our cars, okay? You are my friend and we are shopping for flowers for our families, okay?" Cedric joins the play. You remain nearby to offer play support and guidance until it appears they have accepted Cedric into their play and Cedric has assumed the role they suggested. ‡

Helping Children Develop the Skill of Affiliation

- ❍ Assist the child in parallel play with others.
- ❍ Tutor the child in skills necessary for cooperative play.
- ❍ Stay with the child during the learning phase.
- ❍ Teach words needed to play with others.
- ❍ Help children accept rather than exclude the child that is learning.
- ❍ Teach ways for children to play together.
- ❍ Create a sense of partnership in the room.
- ❍ Help children discuss ways to make the group feel like a "family."
- ❍ Provide many activity choices that require two-or-three children to work together to accomplish them.
- ❍ Teach children how to create and protect friendships. ⁂

dren with the same feelings. This affiliation becomes unhealthy because they join together based on negative feelings about themselves.

The practitioner's role in helping children learn to join a playgroup is crucial. Instead of urging the class to play with a child who is still learning the skills of self-regulation and affiliation, provide many opportunities for joining with others in activities. Begin by promoting positive parallel play. Once children have accomplished this solitary play, they are ready to learn how to join others. Provide play tutoring and guidance to teach them the skills necessary for social play. Children learn the skills necessary for social play and affiliation through practice, so foster many partner play opportunities. Redirect any exclusionary behaviors on the part of children. Ensure a sense of community and partnerships in your classrooms through conversation and attentive relationships with the children. Vivian Paley taught this skill using a class guideline of "You can't say you can't play" (Paley, 1992). Involve children in discussions about how to make the classroom or center feel like a family. Provide many activity choices that require two-or-three children to accomplish. Finally help children create, foster, and protect their friendships and the friendships of others.

Awareness

One of the goals in early childhood education has always been to help young children become accepting, encouraging, and aware of others around them. Practitioners use "feeling" words to help children acknowledge and identify the feelings of others. In addition, they foster in children the ability to show empathy toward classmates through their actions and teaching strategies. Child development theory informs practitioners how children as young as two years old can show concern for others.

Child development experts agree that for a child to be able to understand the feelings of another, she must have some level of cognitive and emotional development. Beginning in the preschool years, empathy, or awareness, is a skill that supports the social development on which early childhood practitioners focus. However, the groundwork for these behaviors begins in infancy. Even newborn babies tend to cry when they hear the cries of other babies. Although instinctive, this demonstration of early empathy development is fostered when adults engage in face-to-face communication with infants. These "conversations" between adults and infants promote attachment that must develop before children can empathize with a hurting friend intentionally. True empathy awareness requires that children recognize they are separate from other people. Child development specialists have shown that children nearing age two begin to empathize with others even going so far as to comfort the other child with a stuffed animal, blanket, or pacifier.

Factors Involved in the Development of Awareness. This emotional/cognitive skill of awareness begins back at the stage of attachment. Child developmentalists have shown that children with healthy attachment as babies are more socially competent and empathetic as four-year-olds. This connection to earlier stages of emotional development is important. It demonstrates that the work in early childhood, beginning at birth, affects the emotional development of the child later in life.

The ability to recognize the needs, interests, and value of others is directly related to the development of a healthy attachment and ability to regulate one's own emotions. If attachment, self-regulation, and affiliation are developed, children begin to "read" the needs of others by watching their faces and actions, listening to them, and forming friendships with them. If a child has developed an ability to join with others (affiliation), she begins to see ways that children are alike and different. Practitioners can foster the development of affiliation by helping children avoid labels and stereotypes. By doing so, practitioners help children become less likely to exclude others, tease others, or act aggressively toward others who are different.

As stated earlier, the development of awareness is tied to cognitive ability and temperament. Therefore, adult styles of teaching that are nurturing and encouraging are the best techniques for fostering the skills related to awareness because the model conveys and teaches acceptance of and respect for others. This modeling at times must be intentional and even taught by practitioners, especially to children who struggle with self-regulation and affiliation. The following vignette demonstrates the intentional teaching of acceptance and respect.

"You can't play with us Jesse, you always hit. Teacher, Jesse is by us!" The practitioner must redirect this kind of interaction by immediately intervening, "Sara, tell Jesse and me what you mean." Sara explains, "Teacher, Jesse always hits, I don't want her here. She can't play." Paraphrase, "Sara, you think Jesse is coming here to hit you?" Sara exclaims, "Yes!" "Jesse, are you over here by the kitchen and babies because you want to hit Sara?" the practitioner asks. Jesse assures them, "No teacher, I want to play babies and she said I can't play." Sara argues, "Jesse, you always hit me when you play, 'cuz you don't like how I play." The practitioner lets the children continue to talk this out until they need help, new words, or a suggestion of a solution. She suggests, "Jesse, I wonder if you want to tell Sara about what you want to do with her." Jesse explains, "Teacher, I want to play with her." The practitioner helps Jesse direct her comments, "Jesse, tell Sara." Jesse responds, "Sara, I want to play babies with you."

The practitioner can help Sara see a "new" Jesse—someone who is learning new play skills and awareness of others' feelings. "Sara, it sounds to me like Jesse would really like to try again with you. What are you pretending today?" Sara says, "I'm pretending that my grandma is coming to visit and I'm making supper for her." The teacher responds, "Oh, that sounds like fun, Sara! Do you have someone to be the grandma?" Sara shakes her head, "No." The practitioner suggests, "I have an idea, Sara. You could ask Jesse to be the grandma who is coming to visit you and the baby. What you do think?" Sara is unsure about this but the teacher asks, "Jesse, would you like to be the grandma who is coming to visit Sara and the baby?" Jesse agrees. The teacher asks, "Sara, did you hear that?" She accepts the idea. The practitioner offers play assistance to ensure Sara's empathy toward Jesse and Jesse's emerging self-control by saying, "Well, I could help you two get started and stay until you don't need me anymore."

Once the two children begin playing, the practitioner provides story details, words, and awareness of others as needed.

This kind of assistance by the practitioner teaches both children to avoid stereotypical beliefs that people can never change and exclusionary behaviors. The results are children who learn to accept, forgive, and encourage.

Tolerance and Respect

Healthy emotional development is the basis for all interactions with and reactions to people. When children have moved along the developmental continuum in this area, they begin to develop tolerance and respect for people because they can regulate their strong feelings, get along with those not quite like them, and empathize with their needs. The previous skills that have been described set the stage for tolerance.

When children and adults encounter a new idea, a new situation, or a new person, the first instinct is to figure out how their own ideas or reality fit with the new one. Without healthy emotional development, fears, frustrations, and lack of empathy can result where friendliness, cooperation, and empathy could have been. In this situation, confronting a new idea, a child with strong self-regulatory and affiliation skills can calm herself to take in the new ideas and understand how she "fits" with them. A healthy awareness of others helps her accept that new ideas are "allowed" and can be held by others. This acceptance leads her to learning a tolerance and respect for others and their ideas without feeling threatened or angry.

Factors Involved in the Development of Tolerance and Respect. The most important factor related to the development of tolerance and respect is the development of the other emotional skills presented in this chapter. If children miss one, it affects their ability to develop the next. The work of the early childhood practitioner builds the foundation for the emotional/social skills of the third grader. Practitioners must observe the child's developmental levels and provide assistance to proceed to the next level.

Understanding Children's Temperament Traits

Parenting styles, strategies of early childhood practitioners, and children's temperaments influence the development of the emotional stages presented so far in this chapter. Early childhood practitioners must understand how temperament traits affect children's emotional development and reaction to social interactions and learn how to match their strategies to each child's individual temperament.

Children's temperament traits "wire" them for dealing with emotions and social interactions. The following definitions of temperament traits are a good start to understanding children, but observations of children by the practitioner, information from the parents, and records of trial and error—what works and doesn't work with each child—are all important aspects of gaining an "understanding" about each child.

Activity Level

Children have certain active and inactive periods throughout the day. Some children are always in motion, some aren't. Practitioners can determine the activity level of children by comparing their active to inactive times. The responsiveness of the practitioner to a child's activity level can enhance the relationship and resulting development. If the child is a "slow mover," the practitioner matches her activity level by using a calm voice, smiles, and gentle movements.

Gender must be considered here. Typically, boys engage in more active play, superhero play, and rough and tumble play. In an area of education dominated by female teachers, this high activity level of boys can and does interfere with a positive relationships between teacher and child and with emotional development for the boys. Let's be clear here, there are some girls who need just as much active and rough and tumble play as boys, but the overwhelming group engaging in this play and actually needing this play is boys (King and Gartrell, 2004).

Distractibility

Activities taking place around a child can distract her from her own activity. The amount of distractibility displayed by a child can determine her distractibility level. Some babies will stop crying when they are hungry if they are offered a pacifier; others will keep crying. Some preschool children are easily distracted by activities near them, while others can concentrate through almost anything. Knowledge of a child's distractibility level is important. Babies who aren't comforted by a pacifier if they are hungry will just be frustrated and anxious if the practitioner continues to try this method of soothing. Preschoolers who find it difficult to concentrate at large group time with many children sitting near them talking, whispering, or moving while the teacher is sharing, display inattentiveness or behaviors that disrupt because they are distracted.

Persistence

This temperament trait is the same thing as the child's attention span. Even babies can have a long attention span. Some will watch a mobile above their crib for a long time, but others will give it just a glance. Early childhood practitioners in preschool settings typically point out the deficit in this trait when children "flit" from one play center to another. What some might think is a delay in development of a longer attention span could actually just be a child's natural temperament. It's important to know the difference before matching teaching strategies. Knowing the difference involves getting to know the child. Practitioners gain information about children by observing them at play, engaging in play with them, and talking with their parents about how they see their child. Once this information is gathered, practitioners can match their strategies to a child's distractibility level (or attention span).

Vygotskians would suggest *shared activities* as a teaching strategy to sustain play and scaffold learning in a way that creates a desire on the child's part to stay with the activity.

Adaptability

This trait defines the child's ability to adjust to changes in the environment. It bears repeating that the responsiveness of the practitioner to children's temperament traits can create a pleasant experience for the children. It is typically stress free and pleasant to care for children who adjust to almost any change in their environment. However, practitioners who understand the need for some children to have a calm environment, where change is minimal, can provide an environment that will ease the child's fear or distress.

Approachability/Withdrawal
Children respond to new objects or new people in different ways. Practitioners typically introduce new ideas, objects, people, and activities to the children in their care. Learning is created when children are exposed to new things. Along with these exciting strategies, knowledge about each child's approachability is important in a responsive setting. Children who refuse to "get messy" withdraw from activities such as finger painting. A responsive practitioner will offer a paintbrush to ease the child's negative response to the activity while encouraging her participation in the painting.

Intensity
This trait is the amount of energy in a child's response to stimulus. It's the loudness of their cry, the energy in their laugh, the intensity of their fear. Early childhood practitioners must find the best response to a child's sadness, joy, and fear that relates well to her emotions. This can take a bit of trial-and-error on the part of the practitioner but is lessened when the parents are included. Including parents begins the moment the child joins the setting. Practitioners must converse with parents about the child's temperament, reactions to new things and people, favorite positions to be held in or to sleep in, and how the child reacts when she's hungry or tired and the best responses to those reactions.

Regularity
A child's innate temperament even measures the regularity of her bodily functions. Sleep schedules, eating schedules, napping schedules differ for all children. Responsive practitioners are flexible in their scheduling, allowing for individual differences in schedules by offering varied toddler napping times, feeding infants on an "as needed basis," and keeping snacks available for hungry preschoolers who need to eat 45 minutes before lunch is served because morning snack was early.

Sensory Threshold

Some babies startle the instant the lights come on. Others barely seem to notice the change. This intensity of reactions to stimulation indicates the child's sensory threshold. As mentioned, it's important to find out about the child's temperament from the parents. But, to be respectful of each child's "sensory threshold," best practices include: getting the child's attention with your voice; saying you'd like to pick her up; asking her if she'd like to be held; or telling her you'd like to change her diaper. It's less startling if the child receives some sort of warning before disrupting her.

Mood

By determining the amount of a child's joyful behaviors as compared to unhappy behaviors, the practitioner can understand the child's mood type. While it may seem like a "good" vs. "bad" mood, it isn't. Mood type is part of a child's personality. Helping children enjoy activities and play, especially if they are typically fussy or prone to crying, can begin to help them see that they can be happy and have fun. Responsive practitioners don't force this, but ease into it by following the child's lead and remaining calm and caring.

Early childhood practitioners must always match their strategies to a child's temperament. This "goodness of fit" is always the responsibility of the practitioner. Choosing developmentally appropriate practices and floor time activities that match the child's needs, interests, and temperament create a goodness of fit that fosters healthy emotional development.

Creating strong relationships with the child's parents leads to even more strategies that best fit the child. Early childhood practitioners must make this a part of their practice, as well. The following sections present ideas to help the practitioner in these areas.

Developmentally Appropriate Practices

The National Association for the Education of Young Children published its third edition of Developmentally Appropriate Practices in Early Childhood Programs (Bredekamp and Copple) in 2009. This position statement and guidebook support specific practices that match a child's developmental level and temperament traits. Strategies include developmental activities for children, activities shared between practitioners and children, and development of positive relationships with parents. What is important for early childhood practitioners is how the practices and rationale in this guidebook support the practices necessary to create healthy emotional and social development in young children. Each stage of early childhood is presented below along with strategies for developmentally appropriate activities, floor time activities, and the development of positive relationships with parents.

Responsive Practice With Infants

Infants' first experiences with the world revolve around the people who give them care. In daily interactions with their parents and early childhood practitioners, infants begin to trust those adults and develop emotional security. Twenty years of brain research has provided support for strong, secure attachments to a nurturing practitioner can help a growing child endure the ordinary stresses of daily life. Even though there are a variety of ways to provide warm, consistent care for infants and toddlers, Bredekamp and Copple (1987) in *Developmentally Appropriate Practices in Early Childhood Programs* outline several for teachers and early childhood practitioners.

The practitioner's primary task is to learn each baby's temperament. This includes learning the baby's eating and sleeping patterns, how the baby likes to be held, when the baby wants to be held, what frightens the baby, how the baby likes to play and becoming able to predict what the baby needs and when. The whole process teaches the baby trust and creates a sense of emotional security. Brazelton and Greenspan (2001) support this all-important time of life by pointing out the critical importance of the practitioner's role. "When there are secure, empathetic, nurturing relationships, children learn to be intimate and empathetic and eventually to communicate about their feelings, reflect on their own wishes, and develop their own relationships with peers and adults" (p. 3). These responsive and secure relationships help children develop the ability to regulate their emotions and behavior.

The development of positive relationships between parents and practitioners is necessary for emotional/social development. Practitioners reinforce the parent's role as their child's first teacher and primary advocate when they stress the importance of daily communication with parents of infants. This communication helps develop trust be-

Floor Time Strategies

Sidney Greenspan has identified five steps in Floor Time that support emotional/social development in young children.

STEP ONE: OBSERVATION. Both listening to and watching a child are necessary for effective observation. Facial expressions, tone of voice, gestures, body posture, and words (or lack of words) are all-important clues that help you determine how to approach the child.

STEP TWO: APPROACH—OPEN CIRCLES OF COMMUNICATION. Once a child's mood and style are known, the practitioner can approach the child with the best words and gestures. The practitioner can open the circle of communication with a child by acknowledging the child's emotional tone and building on whatever interests the child.

STEP THREE: FOLLOW THE CHILD'S LEAD. Following a child's lead means being a supportive play partner who is an "assistant" to the child and allows the child to set the tone, direct the action, and create the story. This gives the child a feeling that "I can have an impact on the world." As the adult continues to support the child's play, the child benefits from the sense of warmth, responsiveness, and understanding from the adult.

STEP FOUR: EXTEND AND EXPAND PLAY. Extending and expanding a child's play themes involves making supportive comments about the child's play without taking control. This helps the child express her own ideas and direct the play story. Asking questions to foster creative thinking can keep the story going, while helping the child understand the emotional themes involved. For example, suppose a child is crashing a car. Rather than asking, "Why are those cars crashing?" the early childhood practitioner may ask empathetically, "Those cars have so much energy and are moving fast. Are they trying to get somewhere?"

STEP FIVE: CHILD CLOSES THE CIRCLE OF COMMUNICATION. As the practitioner opens the circle of communication by approaching the child, the child closes the circle when the child builds on the adult's comments and gestures with comments and gestures of her own. By building on each other's ideas and gestures, the child begins to appreciate and understand the value of shared communication.

Retrieved from the "Greenspan" Floor Time Model found at: http://www.doh.state.fl.us/alternatesites/cms-kids/providers/early_steps/training/documents/floor_time.pdf tween the two. Another reward of this relationship is that when either adult finds a new strategy that works for the child, the other can use it, too. This creates stability and strengthens the infant's ability to trust the responses from both parent and practitioner. When babies can do this, they begin to build trust in their environment. The trust builds the development of attachment and the attachment supports the development of autonomy (independence), which, in turn, helps them feel secure and confident in their ability to make choices and to learn.

The Greenspan method of interaction, called "Floor Time," encourages and demonstrates how to enter the child's activities and follow her lead. It is a warm and personal way of relating with a child. This philosophy encompasses best practices such as engaging, respecting and getting in tune with the child in order to help the child communicate—through gestures, words, and pretend play—what is on the child's mind. As a method of interaction, Floor Time is a five-step process that is used to support the social/emotional development of the child. It is also a helpful technique when working with a child who has special needs because the one-on-one interaction provides the individual attention necessary for the child's learning.

In infancy specifically, Floor Time techniques that encourage attachment and healthy emotional development include "tuning in" and following the child's interests. Tuning in is as simple as getting down on the floor with the child or holding her and beginning a "conversation." From there, the practitioner's job is to figure out what the child would like to do by offering a couple of toys to see if she's interested or playing a game such a "peek-a-boo." A "tuned in" practitioner will carefully work to understand the child's temperament or mood at the time, figure out what she's likely to do, engage in conversation with the child, let the child lead the activity by watching for clues that she's tired, wants to try something else, wants to be held, or wants to be on her own for a while. The "tuned in" practitioner will let the child direct the play by following what she does. For example, the practitioner could hand her a rattle and let her figure out how to use it, let the child stop the activity rather than doing so and encourage the child to "talk" by copying the child's coos, smiles, and body movements. Specific games such as "I'm going to get you" and "pat-a-cake" are perfect floor time strategies for this age.

Responsive Practice With Toddlers

Toddlers are busy learning to be safe, to share/take turns, to use words to express their feelings, and to act appropriately in different situations. They are fascinated by words and the social world. If toddlers experience warm, responsive, consistent care as infants, they learn to be more caring with their peers. If they received responsive, "give and take" care early in life they learned about connecting emotionally with other people. Finally the practitioner who works with toddlers builds on the consistent care that the infant practitioner provided. By helping the child develop healthy, trusting attachments, this give toddlers chances to choose and lead their own play and experience success in figuring things out for themselves. When this kind of encouraging environment and respect is present in the toddler setting, the children will develop confidence and emotional/social competence.

Conversation that enables toddlers to feel in control and gives them new words when needed promotes emotional development. When practitioners initiate a conversation with a toddler, they should give the child ample time to respond. Even though this is a slow process and children of this age have limits in their cognitive and emotional development, they also have a large ability to learn, think, reason, remember, and problem solve. Conversation with an adult provides new words they need to express what they learn, feel, and want. Practitioners must make conversation and learning words a priority when they work with toddlers. Words are key to expressing their strong feelings and needs. When children can do this they eliminate a lot of the need to "act out" to get the same messages across to others.

Practitioners can provide the best for children of this age if they are knowledgeable about developmental expectations and communicate with parents about each child's current level of development. Practitioners ask parents what sounds and words their toddler uses so that they will understand what the child is saying. Partnering with parents in this way ensures a continuity of development because both parents and practitioners are focusing on the same words and phrases.

Practitioners must learn individual temperament traits that toddlers possess. When practitioners match activities to the toddler's needs, interests and temperament traits, social and emotional development can be promoted. Specific strategies that encourage this development and learning include: having correct expectations for toddlers based on their developmental level; watching to see what the child is trying to do; and providing the needed assistance to help the child accomplish the task, allowing the child to do what they can do on their own. Practitioners demonstrate their understanding of toddlers' limited language by responding quickly to their cries or other signs of distress. Once the child has calmed, the practitioner teaches the words the toddler needs to communicate her needs.

Greenspan's *Floor Time* (2002) strategies center on letting the child take the lead. In toddlerhood, joining in a child's play takes a certain skill. If the child wants to stack blocks, practitioners will join the child in her activity with the purpose of developing an emotional connection and interaction. If the practitioner insists that the child join in an adult-planned activity, often the interaction produces a reaction that is centered on pleasing the adult rather than creating play or a connection with the adult. A mutual, child-initiated or led, shared activity engages the child and practitioner in communication. For example, the practitioner might begin to take turns with the child stacking blocks, each stacking one at a time, until the child begins to expect and wait for the practitioner to take a turn. Then, as a way of encouraging emotion and communication, the practitioner might "accidentally" place a block in the wrong spot, coaxing the child to correct the "error." Greenspan considers this extension and expansion of the play to be tuning into the child's imagination and ideas and taking them one step further through gestures and words. The child begins to communicate her ideas through this play and learns to express wants, needs, fantasies, and ideas. The practitioner should gently insist that the child respond to playful interactions and prompting during play. These interactions support emotional and cognitive development. An important part of this interaction always includes letting children end the conversation or activity on their own, when they are ready.

Responsive Practice with Preschoolers

The emotional and social foundation developed in infancy and toddlerhood is the foundation necessary for teaching social play skills in the preschool years. The early warm, consistent, attachment-forming care leads to a child's sense of autonomy and, then, confidence in trying new things. The ability to branch out, try new things, and feel safe in making mistakes is at the core of a play environment. It's in these years when the core emotional strengths of attachment, self-regulation, and affiliation are important.

In this kind of play, a developmentally appropriate philosophy becomes apparent. This play teaches children about symbols, problem solving, conflict resolution, taking turns and making choices. Learning how to play with others is the foundation for interacting with others through grade school and into adulthood. Learning social play skills creates further cognitive and emotional development in the preschool years. If the learning is within a play environment where play activities are self-selected and self-directed by the child, self-satisfying for the child, and facilitated by the practitioner, then they fit the description of developmentally appropriate. These play skills must be taught and supported by the early childhood practitioner.

Learning Play Skills. The idea that preschoolers might need to learn play skills isn't always promoted to early childhood practitioners, rather it is assumed that these skills are naturally acquired. Many children do acquire them naturally, but some do not. The shy, withdrawn children or those who show some aggression may need more help. The first role the practitioner has in children's play is teaching them how to play. If practitioners can help children learn to play, they are giving them a gift for life and an emotional boost.

Children who are shy or slow-to-warm-up can benefit when the practitioner plays next to the child making comments about their own play rather than what the child is doing. This strategy can help children whose persistence is short-tioner can join the play by asking for instructions from the children and following them carefully without directing or taking over. Sometimes, this is enough assistance to help the children move beyond their repetitive play and extend their story and length of play. The benefit of such intervention on the part of the adult is the increased length of the play, the higher cognitive function necessary for the expanded story line, and the affiliation necessary for the children to continue contributing to the group.

For a child with a spirited temperament who wants to engage in social play, the practitioner may need to join the play by offering some control to the children until they all can help her learn the play role she needs to be a part of the group. Once she has learned the role and the other children are "on board," the play scene will serve to help her control her behavior in a way that real life cannot. In other words, in play, a child is capable of more mature behavior than in everyday life. In play, children must conform to the rules of the play situation. The rules surface naturally in play—children don't act anyway they please. One unstated rule might be that a player must stay within her role by using appropriate gestures or even language. As a result, play helps children practice self-regulation.

Promoting Play. Promoting play becomes an advocacy and communication role for the practitioners. Sometimes other practitioners want to know how we think play activities really help children learn. Par-

---

IMAGINE a child who is playing fire fighter with a group of others on the climber. Her assigned role in the play is to lie still until rescuers arrive. This same child typically finds it impossible to sit still in a circle time, but this play that she has joined willingly supports her self-regulation to a point that she can lie perfectly still for five minutes. The play itself and the rules and roles of that social play have enabled that child to perform at a level not typical for her at other times. The play scenario is actually assisting her to regulate her behavior much longer than she could on her own. ✥

ents often ask how early childhood practitioners can teach through play. Promoting play involves communication with others, especially parents. They typically want to know two things: first, that the practitioner has a plan for their child and second, that the practitioner knows early childhood theory and best practice. The role of the early childhood practitioner is to help parents see how the classroom has been developed around children's development and the goal is to help children develop socially and emotionally, while learning to learn, learning to trust their instincts, learning to discover, and learning to get their ideas across. Play provides the opportunity for this important learning to take place.

Greenspan's *Floor Time* (2002) strategies help support the play skills in preschoolers. His ideas for expanding abstract thinking support the best practices related to teaching play described here. It is important to follow the child's lead and build on her ideas. Practitioners can expand play skills by encouraging fantasy, recognizing fears and avoidance of certain feelings or themes, helping children identify problems or plots in the play, and accepting all feelings, thus, encouraging empathy.

By using *Floor Time* (2002) techniques and play teaching strategies, the responsive practitioner helps children develop play skills that foster self-regulation, affiliation, and awareness of others.

EVEN when preschoolers choose their own play settings and ideas, sometimes they need help choosing a plot or storyline for their play. The observant practitioner watches to see if play assistance is necessary. If it appears that the children are loosing focus, beginning to disagree, or the play begins to fall apart, the practitioner can join the play as a tutor. The practitioner can ask about their story, find out who is doing what, and then help by suggesting new roles and leading the children in a discussion about the way they want the play to go. Once they have made the decisions about the play, the practitioner stays as a co-player just until it is clear that the children can continue alone. At that point, the practitioners can move away from the play to observe. This kind of strategy encourages problem-solving, play skill development, creativity, and conversation. ‡

What About Upsetting Behaviors?

Many times, a child's temperament or strong, unmet needs can also create behaviors that upset other children and the practitioners. The child displaying the behavior is at the same time experiencing a wealth of upsetting emotions. These behaviors can leave the practitioner and child frustrated and exhausted. It's important to always remember that the behavior is a reaction by the child to activities or transitions that are upsetting due to her temperament; to strong unmet needs that can be physical or emotional; to lack of language skills; or to something as simple as fatigue.

The practitioner's role is four-fold: understanding the child's temperament; asking the parent if the child is experiencing illness or other needs, including sleep and feeding needs; matching developmentally appropriate practices to the child's interests and developmental levels; and engaging the child in conversation and play, always following the child's lead.

In infancy and toddlerhood, upsetting behaviors include crying and physical reactions to others due to lack of language skills needed to get their needs met, or strong emotional or physical needs. The practitioner must be observant, responsive, caring, and consistent in her role with the children in an effort to understand them, teach them, calm them, and provide for them. Daily information from parents about their child's mood, physical health, amount of sleep, etc., is crucial here.

In preschool, upsetting behaviors include those mentioned above and for many of the same reasons. Remember, a preschooler may still have language delays or other health or developmental issues similar to a toddler. Other reasons include mismatch of activities to the child's temperament or interests, strong emotional needs resulting from slower emotional development, or parenting styles. The role of the practitioner is the same: know the child, partner with the parent, adjust practices, and create activities that meet her needs.

Sometimes, the practitioner's role involves teaching children ways of settling disputes. No child enters play planning on having a fight. The disputes evolve from misunderstandings such as lack of verbal skills to express needs, strong feelings about the play, lack of space, or lack of equipment. The practitioner must help children learn to negotiate—it truly is one of the great benefits of play. As much as possible, let children solve on their own, give them words as needed and teach the words necessary.

Violent themes in play can be a practitioner's worst nightmare. Violent play is when children's play interactions emulate violent models. Play is at its most immature level here. Children are unable in this kind of play to control emotional reactions. They cannot follow even simple play rules. Solutions that can be taught by the practitioner include suggesting other roles that can be just as interesting, helping children work it out, asking questions about the play, and redirecting the play to a new play theme.

Summary

Practitioners must have knowledge of general social and emotional development to be able to best meet the needs of each child. Understanding typical developmental milestones is the start to forming strategies, classroom environments, and learning goals for children. Additionally and most importantly, they must understand and respect individual differences in each child in their care. The practitioner must observe each child's behaviors in an effort to recognize her strengths, emerging skills, and work areas. This is one of the steps in the adult's role of individualizing expectations and strategies for social and emotional development.

Creating partnerships with parents is another key step. When practitioners place a strong emphasis on creating positive relationships with parents, everyone wins. Parents share frustrations, describe emerging skills and goals that they have for their children during discussions with the early childhood practitioner. Parents learn that the practitioner, and, as a result, the early childhood setting is focused on the family and desires to create relationships with them. The message they receive is that they are valued as the most important person in their child's life—their input not only matters, it is sought. When parents receive this message and see it practiced, they become active partners in their child's care and learning. This relationship creates an early childhood environment and program that facilitates positive social and emotional development.

Early childhood practitioners have a critical role in infants' emotional development. Their responsive, warm, consistent care of the infants supports the development of such skills as self-awareness, handling strong feelings, showing empathy, and practicing social competence. Specific practices include gentle, supportive, responsive, and nurturing interactions; many one-to-one, face-to-face interactions (play and conversation) with the infants; many interactions throughout the day; consistent responses and frequent adjustments to infants' individual feeding and sleeping schedules; attentiveness to infants during caregiving routines; and warm greetings to infants and their parents each day.

A child's first experiences with the world revolve around the people closest to him. In daily interactions with her parents and early childhood practitioner, she begins to trust those adults and develop emotional security. This attachment and consistent care teaches the baby trust and creates a sense of emotional security. This trust and emotional security are crucial for play skills and confidence in exploring and discovering during the toddler and preschool years. In fact, these emotional connections are the baby's first ways of getting to know the world and setting the stage for cognitive development. These connections help children develop an ability to regulate their emotions and behavior. Daily communication between parents and practitioners helps develop trust.

Practitioners help toddlers learn words through initiating conversations and giving the children plenty of time to answer or reply with a response. Reading books and playing with toddlers can create natural opportunities for these conversations. Parents can provide important information about their children's language development. Practitioners must ask parents what sounds and words their toddler uses so they can extend conversations using those words. Children in toddlerhood require support from their practitioners, helping them to accomplish tasks, but allowing the child to do what they are capable of doing on their own. Practitioners must quickly help toddlers with limited language skills when their cries of frustration or anger or fear signal the need. The quick response continues to build the emotional attachment and trust.

Supporting the developing self-concept and social skills of preschoolers is the job of early childhood practitioners. They must create and maintain and encourage children to develop confidence and competence, not by being told how wonderful or special they are, but by being given chances to take initiative, experience success, and figure things out for themselves. Promoting play skills that ultimately teach social skills is an advocacy role that is a large part of the early childhood practitioner's role.

KEY POINTS

1. The emotional development of children is ongoing. Children develop emotionally through a sequence of stages. There are several milestones for ongoing emotional development in children. It is important for practitioners to understand these milestones so they have appropriate expectations.

2. Six key strengths have been identified that young children need to develop. They include: attachment, self-regulation, affiliation, awareness, tolerance, and respect.

3. Children are born with innate temperament styles that make them unique and have an impact on their behavior. It is the role of practitioners to observe and understand each child's temperament. Practitioners must work to match their teaching styles to the toleration needs of the individual.

4. Practitioners need to work with parents to create a partnership in building a child's healthy emotional development. Practitioners can create trusting relationships by asking questions about the child, honoring the parenting skills, inviting shared problem solving, and requesting information about the child's emerging social and emotional development.

5. Early childhood practitioners support and promote play as a means by which young children develop emotionally, socially, and cognitively. Practitioners working with infants support the development of attachment and trust which are the foundations for self-regulation and social play skills. Those working with toddlers provide opportunities for language development, support attempts at social skills, and respond quickly to frustrations. They extend toddlers play and move a child from parallel to more social play. Practitioners working with preschoolers recognize the role they play in helping children learn to engage in cooperative group play.

6. Floor Time is a philosophy that embraces the relationship between adults and children in an atmosphere of caring. By observing, opening circles of communication, following the child's lead, extending and expanding the child's play, and letting the child bring play to a close, practitioners support the emotional and social development of young children.

REFERENCES

Gartrell, D. (2004). *The Power of Guidance.* Clifton Park, NY: Thomson Publishers.

Greenspan, S. *The Greenspan Floor Time Model* [PDF document]. Retrieved from Florida Department of Health Web Site: http://www.doh.state.fl.us/alternatesites/cms-kids/providers/early_steps/training/documents/floor_time.pdf

Copple, C., & Bredekamp, S. (Eds.) (2009). *Developmentally Appropriate Practice in Early Childhood Programs. (3rd ed.).* Washington, DC: NAEYC.

Brazelton, T. B. and Greenspan, S. (2000). *The Irreducible Needs of Children—What Every Child Must Have to Grow, Learn, and Flourish.* Cambridge, MA: Perseus Publishing.

Perry, B. *Train the Trainer Series 2 Six Core Strengths for Healthy Child Development* [PDF document]. Retrieved from Centre for Children and Families in the Justice System Web site: http://www.lfcc.on.ca/Perry_Six_Core_Strengths.pdf

Paley, V. (1993). *You Can't Say You Can't Play.* Harvard University Press.

PART 2

Observation and Assessment: Strategies for Inclusion

CHAPTER 4

Observation:
Finding the Function
of Behavior

Dr. Melissa Olive

Introduction

YOUNG children have engaged in problem behaviors for many years and for just as many years, those problem behaviors have served a purpose for children. In fact, the earliest study in which researchers tried to alter a young child's behavior dates back to the mid 1960s.

In this study, a young child engaged in crawling behavior when she had the ability to walk. She crawled because crawling resulted in higher rates of attention from staff that verbally reminded her to walk (Harris, Johnston, Kelley, and Wolf, 1964). Historically, behavior guidance approaches were attempted in this manner by reacting to or attempting to punish challenging behavior. These strategies often came in the form of reprimands (e.g., "no hitting") or mild punishers (e.g., time out) following the form (e.g., hit) of the behavior. Little time or attention was given to observing behaviors, particularly the events and information surrounding behaviors.

Research has shown that these punishment approaches may be effective temporarily but in the long-term have negative effects on children (Sobsey, 1990). One long-term effect of punishment is that it could cause the child to have a negative relationship with the person who delivers the punishment. A second negative effect of punishment is that it could cause the child to act out the behavior on other children.

A third negative effect of punishment is that it can cause the behavior to increase rather than decrease.

As researchers learned the negative effects of punishment, they began studying alternative approaches to behavior guidance. This new research has suggested that practitioners should attend to outcomes of children's behavior rather than forms of behavior. Thus, form is what behaviors look like and outcomes are what behaviors get. For example, Suzie hits her friend Tom in housekeeping. Tom begins to cry and leaves the housekeeping area. In this example, hitting is the form and Tom crying and leaving housekeeping are the outcomes or "payoff" of the behavior. In the crawling example previously mentioned, crawling is the form of the behavior and the attention she got for crawling was the outcome.

Another word for outcomes, or "payoffs," is function. Essentially, there are two primary functions of behavior. Children get or obtain something they prefer or they avoid or escape something they do not like. In general, things children obtain or avoid can be classified into four categories: objects, activities, attention, and sensations. See Figure 1 for more examples of functions of children's challenging behavior.

Indirect Assessments

Just as children grow and develop individually, each child engages in challenging behavior for individual reasons. One way to determine why children engage in challenging behavior is to conduct a functional behavioral assessment (FBA). This assessment helps practitioners determine the function, the outcome, or the payoff for the challenging behavior. The three steps in an FBA are indirect assessments, direct assessments, and functional analysis.

Indirect assessments consist of important tools that help gather information before the direct assessment portion of the FBA is completed. Indirect assessments are called such because they can be done without observing the child. Practitioners complete indirect assessments by gathering information from the child's parents, previous caregivers, or extended family members. Indirect assessments can come in many forms. Interviews are one type of indirect assessment. A practitioner might interview parents about when India's challenging behavior occurs at home. She could call India's van driver and interview him about what happens after challenging behavior occurs on the van. She could phone India's speech therapist and ask what sets off challenging behavior during speech therapy.

Figure 1.

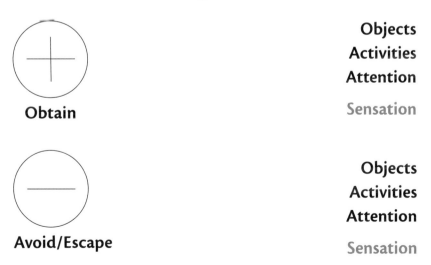

Obtain

Objects
Activities
Attention
Sensation

Avoid/Escape

Objects
Activities
Attention
Sensation

Rating scales are another type of indirect assessment. The Motivational Assessment Scale (MAS; Durand and Crimmins, 1990) is a popular rating scale used in the FBA process. The MAS consists of a questionnaire that requires the rater to rank if the behavior never occurs to always occurs for 16 different situations. After the questions are answered, the answers are transferred to a score sheet and the behaviors are classified into one of several functions. A modified MAS for early childhood is included in Appendix A.

Another rating scale that has been used for indirect assessments is the Question About Behavior Function (QABF: Matson and Vollmer, 1995). In this measure, raters answer 25 questions regarding the target behavior. Each question is rated for frequency as well as severity. Scores are summed to obtain possible functions of targeted challenging behavior. The QABF has been reported to have higher agreement among raters (Nicholson, Konstantinidi, and Furniss, 2006) as well as higher agreement with direct observation results (Paclawskyj, Matson, Rush, Smalls, and Vollmer, 2001).

In summary, indirect assessments help practitioners prepare for direct assessments by assessing what people think about the following:

▶ When challenging behaviors occur
▶ What happens before behaviors
▶ What happens after behaviors
▶ What challenging behaviors looks like

Indirect assessments are also helpful in determining why other people think challenging behaviors occur.

Direct Observation

When practitioners begin to complete direct assessments, they should write down observations of behavior. While memory is good for some things, by the end of the day, practitioners might forget key components of the day such as who was present when Sally pulled hair or exactly what happened after Marissa screamed during art. Documenting behaviors in writing is most important because later, those records will be available when it is time to summarize assessment information.

Practitioners should take great care to be objective when writing

down observations of student behavior, noting only the observable
facts. It might be difficult to remain objective after observing
a child hit, especially if there
is an injury that requires immediate attention. However,
subjective notes—those that
contain feelings or judgments
about a situation—might mis-
construe assessment data and
should be avoided at all times.

Of course, it is not necessary to
write down everything. Practitioners would
have time for nothing else! One recommended method for recording
behaviors is called the ABCs of behavior. It gets its name because the
three things to be recorded are antecedents, behaviors, and consequences. The A stands for antecedents, the B stands for behavior, and
the C stands for consequences (Bijou, Peterson, and Ault, 1968).

As previously described, children engage in behaviors for reasons,
payoffs, or functions. In fact, all behavior occurs for a reason, even typical adult behavior. For example, if Mariah walks into a dark room, she
turns on the light, and the light comes on. Or if Zane drives his car and
sees the stop sign, he stops the car. As a result, he avoids a car accident
or a traffic citation. If Patricio sits at a restaurant and the server walks
up, she orders her food. As a result, her food comes. If Jamison has a
headache, he takes an aspirin. As a result the headache goes away. All of
these examples demonstrate how behavior occurs naturally in the daily environment. Each of these examples has an antecedent, behavior,
and consequence. An antecedent occurs, first triggering the behavior
that is followed by a consequence. Consequences are either added or
removed, resulting in people getting outcomes or avoiding outcomes.
See Figure 2 for a better portrayal of the patterns described above.

In many instances, practitioners might also need to note other
important variables in the environment, including who was around,
what was happening, and when and where events occurred. This information is important because patterns could emerge over time.
For example, Josie might only engage in tantrums with her favorite

teacher or during her least-favorite activity. Practitioners should also note patterns within the behavior such as what makes the behavior escalate, what makes the behavior stop, and what makes the behavior start. For example, Chelsea used to cry. However, when her teacher Suzie left the room, she stopped crying. After a few days, Suzie noticed Chelsea followed her to the next room and, then, started crying again! If Suzie had not recorded the behavior for several days, she might not have noticed these patterns of Chelsea's behaviors. One version of an ABC form is included in Appendix B for practitioners to use.

Data Analysis

Transfer the Data

After practitioners have recorded several days of observations, those records can be transferred to a separate form to help indicate patterns or trends in the data. The Functional Assessment Direct Observation Form (O'Neil, et al., 1997) was modified and included in Appendix C for practitioners to use. Upon first glance it might appear overwhelming. After a few trials though, it will become much easier to use. A practitioner had a little girl named Maxine in class who had difficulties during circle time. After several days of observation during circle, the practitioner had enough data to begin completing the form. The first day, Maxine hit one of her friends during a song. Her friend cried and the practitioner told her, "No hitting." A few minutes later, one of Maxine's

Figure 2. ABC Analysis

Date Time	Antecedent	Behavior	Consequence	Possible Function
	Room is dark	Mariah turns on light	Light comes on	Obtain object or activity
	See stop sign	Zane stops the car	Avoid traffic citation	Avoid object or activity
	See server at restaurant	Patriccio orders food	Food comes	Obtain object
	Get a headache	Jamison takes a pain reliever	Headache goes away	Avoid or escape a sensation

friends had a turn in circle and Maxine pulled another friend's hair. Then, the teaching assistant came over told Maxine, "No hair pulling!" and sat next to Maxine to supervise more closely. A few minutes later the group was singing a song and Maxine pulled someone's hair and Maxine was told "No" again. As can be seen on Monday, October 10, Maxine engaged in six instances of disruptive behavior during circle. Looking at Tuesday's data and event number seven, Maxine first hit a friend after a different friend got a turn. Maxine was told "No." There were only three instances of behavior on Tuesday. There were four instances of behavior on Wednesday. These are numbered ten, eleven and twelve. As can be seen, she hit, bit, screamed, and ran away. The antecedents were a peer having a turn, singing a song, and physical prompting to participate in movements. The consequences were being told "No" and the teaching assistant sitting next to Maxine.

Make Sense of the Data

After the data are organized, practitioners are ready to analyze data to determine why the challenging behavior is occurring. Several steps are necessary in this process. First, practitioners must determine what initiates the behavior or, in other words, what the antecedents are. Second, practitioners must determine what consequences follow challenging behavior, or what the function is for challenging behavior. Third, practitioners must identify what skills children lack. In many instances, children engage in challenging behavior because they lack other skills. Last, if there are still no clear patterns, it may be necessary to seek additional help from a behavioral expert.

Analyze Antecedents

As stated previously, practitioners must identify what variables precede challenging behavior. This is important for several reasons. Most importantly, practitioners will know when to implement interventions. The antecedent data from the practitioner's observations of Maxine during circle indicate exactly when to implement interventions. Also, antecedent data show practitioners when reinforcers or preferences for children may be lacking. For example, children often engage in challenging behavior because their reinforcers are limited. The antecedent data provide information about when to increase access to those preferred reinforcers.

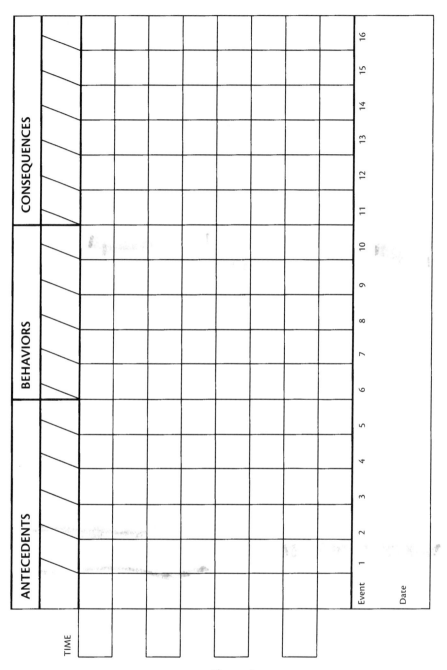

Figure 3.

Melissa L. Olive and Project FACEC. Adapted from O'Neill, R. E., Hamer, R. H., Albin, R. W., Storey, K, and Sprague, J. R. (1997). *Functional Assessment and Program Development for Problem Behavior: A Practical Handbook.* (Second ed.) Pacific Grove: Wadsworth.

Antecedent data also tell practitioners when tasks might be too difficult, confusing, or too easy for children. This information can be used to alter instructional environments to help children become successful. Common antecedents that initiate challenging behavior are transitions between activities or too many transitions in too short of a time span. Other activities that set off challenging behavior are activities that are too difficult, too easy, too long, or too short. Like the famous childhood story, Goldilocks and the Three Bears, early childhood practitioners have to get it "just right."

Practitioners should be able to categorize or summarize their data. For example, as previously discussed, while all Maxine's behavior occurred during circle, almost 50 percent occurred when the group was singing a song. Almost 25 percent occurred when a peer was having a turn. Perhaps, Maxine did not like the songs that were being sung or the songs were too loud. The practitioner also noticed Maxine didn't have as many turns as other children. After Maxine was given choices of songs to sing, the practitioner noticed that Maxine's behaviors decreased during circle. This gave her both choices and turns. Summarizing data into percentages will help practitioners understand better when challenging behavior is occurring and what environmental variables are contributing to challenging behavior.

Analyze Consequences

After antecedents are analyzed, it is equally important to analyze consequences for patterns and trends. This is done in a very similar manner. As previously discussed, Maxine received 100 percent attention from adults when she engaged in challenging behavior. She received 25 percent attention from peers when she engaged in challenging behavior. These data suggest that, most of the time, she received a large amount of attention for her challenging behavior. These data, in combination with the antecedent data, suggest that the function of her challenging behavior was to obtain attention. Chapter Five focuses more on how to design strategies when children seek attention from peers and adults.

Look for Missing Skills

Practitioners should also analyze data to determine if the child is missing important skills. Sometimes, children engage in challenging

behavior because they lack certain skills. For example, challenging behavior can serve as a form of communication, even when a child demonstrates effective communication skills. However, a child who enjoys music might engage in challenging behavior during transitions because she did not understand that music was coming next. Simple cues such as shaking a maraca and "time for music" helped decrease her tantrums during transitions to music. Other skills may include learning how to put shoes on independently, dispensing soap during hand washing, or sharing materials.

Still No Patterns?

Sometimes after practitioners have analyzed all antecedents, consequences, and missing skills, they realize the data has no clear patterns. For example, the data appear jumbled, suggesting sometimes the child gets attention and sometimes she gets escape or a preferred object. If after all the data have been analyzed and there are no clear patterns, it may be helpful to seek the advice of a behavioral consultant to help conduct an additional assessment called a functional analysis. In this third step of the functional behavioral assessment, the consultant helps practitioners manipulate the environment to determine the cause of challenging behavior. For example, if Chuie is engaging in challenging behavior during circle time on Monday, the behavior consultant might suggest that the teacher give Chuie attention after challenging behavior. On Tuesday, Chuie's teacher might give her an escape after challenging behavior such as a short break from circle time. On Wednesday, Chuie's teacher might give her a tangible following challenging behavior. Therefore, on this day Chuie would get a preferred object following challenging behavior. This analysis of behaviors continues until a pattern emerges. The behavior consultant then collects data to determine which day or which consequence resulted in a more challenging behavior. The results of this assessment tell the practitioner and consultant why Chuie is engaging in challenging behavior.

Research on Functional Behavioral Assessment

Recent laws such as the No Child Left Behind Act (2008) have resulted in practitioners attending to and utilizing *Evidenced Based Approaches*. Recently, Wood and colleagues (2009) reviewed studies about challenging behavior in early childhood settings from 1990 through 2007. They reported that young children had benefitted from FBAs and carefully designed interventions. This finding suggests that the use of FBAs in early childhood settings is an evidenced-based approach for practitioners to use in their classrooms.

Summary

In summary, children engage in behaviors for specific reasons: to obtain objects, activities, attention, and sensory or to avoid objects, activities, attention, and sensations. Completing a functional behavioral assessment will help practitioners determine what children are getting from their challenging behavior. Direct observation is a necessary step in this process. Documenting antecedents, behaviors, and consequences as well as important variables such as who, what, when and where provides practitioners with important information as they start to analyze data during the assessment.

KEY POINTS

1. Challenging behavior serves a purpose for children.

2. Practitioners should gather as much information as possible during the functional behavioral assessment (FBA) process.

3. Recording observations in writing is important; memory does not work as well.

4. A variety of tools are available to assist in the FBA process.

5. The ABC chart is one tool that can be used to help understand the relationships between children's behavior and environmental outcomes.

6. Practitioners can alter their own behavior to help meet needs of children.

7. Consider all factors that can contribute to children's challenging behaviors (e.g., too many transitions, over-stimulating environments, inadvertent reinforcement, too difficult tasks, too easy tasks).

8. In some cases, children can be taught new skills that could result in decreases in challenging behavior.

REFERENCES

Bijou, S. W., Peterson, R. F., and Ault, M. H. (1968). "A Method to Integrate Descriptive and Experimental Field Studies at the Level of Data and Empirical Concepts," *Journal of Applied Behavior Analysis, 1*, 175–191.

Durand, V. M. & Crimmins, D. B. (1990). "The Motivational Assessment Scale," *Severe Behavior Problems: A Functional Communication Training Approach.* (V.M. Durand, Ed.) New York: Guilford Press.

Harris, F.R., Johnston, M.K., Kelley, C.S., and Wolf, M.M. (1964). "Effects of Positive Social Reinforcement on Regressed Crawling of a Nursery School Child," *Journal of Educational Psychology, 55*, 35–41.

Matson, J. L., and Vollmer, T. (1995). "Questions About Behavioral Function (QABF)." Baton Rouge, LA: Scientific Publications.

Nicholson, J., Konstantinidi, E., and Furniss, F. (2006). "On Some Psychometric Properties of the Questions about Behavioral Function (QABF) scale," *Research in Developmental Disabilities, 27*, 337–352.

No Child Left Behind Act of 2001, 20 U.S.C. § 6319 (2008).

O'Neill, R. E., Horner, R. H., Albin, R. W., Storey, L., and Sprague, J. R. (1997). *Functional Assessment and Program Development for Problem Behavior: A Practical Handbook.* (2nd ed.) Pacific Grove: Wadsworth.

Paclawskyj, T. R., Matson, J. L., Rush, K. S., Smalls, Y., and Vollmer, T. R. (2001). "Assessment of the Convergent Validity of the Questions About Behavioral Function Scale with Analogue Functional Analysis and the Motivation Assessment Scale." *Journal of Intellectual Disability Research, 45*, 484–494.

Sobsey, D. (1990). "Modifying the Behavior of Behavior Modifiers." In A. Repp & N. Singh (Eds.), *Perspectives on the Use of Nonaversive and Aversive Interventions for Persons with Developmental Disabilities* (pp. 421–433). Sycamore, IL: Sycamore Publishing.

Wood, B. K., Kwang-Sun, C. B., and Ferro, J. B. (2009). "Young Children with Challenging Behavior," *Topics in Early Childhood Special Education, 29*, 68–78.

APPENDIX A.

Motivation Assessment Scale

Adapted For Use By Early Childhood Practitioners

Name _____

Rater _____

Date _____

Behavior Description _____

Setting Description _____

INSTRUCTIONS: The Motivation Assessment Scale is a questionnaire designed to identify those situations in which a child is likely to behave in certain ways. From this information, more informed decisions can be made concerning the selection of particular interest. It is important that you identify the behavior very specifically. Aggressive, for example, is not as good a description as hits his sister. Once you have specified the behavior to be rated, read each question carefully and circle the one number that best describes your observations of this behavior.

Questions

1. Would the child happily engage in this behavior if left alone for long periods of time? (For example, hand flopping or body rocking for 20 minutes.)

2. Does the behavior occur after you ask the child to do something difficult?

3. Does the behavior occur when you are talking to other adults or children in the room?

4. Does the behavior ever occur to get a toy, food, or activity that this child has been told that he or she can't have?

5. Do you think that the behavior would occur repeatedly, in the same way, for very long periods of time, if no one was around? (For example, rocking back and forth for 20 minutes.)

6. Does the behavior occur when you ask the child to do something?

7. Does the behavior occur whenever you stop looking at or talking to the child?

8. Does the behavior occur when you take away a favorite toy, food or activity?

9. Does it appear to you that this child enjoys performing the behavior?

Answers

Never 0	Almost Never 1	Seldom 2	Half the Time 3	Usually 4	Almost Always 5	Always 6
Never 0	Almost Never 1	Seldom 2	Half the Time 3	Usually 4	Almost Always 5	Always 6
Never 0	Almost Never 1	Seldom 2	Half the Time 3	Usually 4	Almost Always 5	Always 6
Never 0	Almost Never 1	Seldom 2	Half the Time 3	Usually 4	Almost Always 5	Always 6
Never 0	Almost Never 1	Seldom 2	Half the Time 3	Usually 4	Almost Always 5	Always 6
Never 0	Almost Never 1	Seldom 2	Half the Time 3	Usually 4	Almost Always 5	Always 6
Never 0	Almost Never 1	Seldom 2	Half the Time 3	Usually 4	Almost Always 5	Always 6
Never 0	Almost Never 1	Seldom 2	Half the Time 3	Usually 4	Almost Always 5	Always 6
Never 0	Almost Never 1	Seldom 2	Half the Time 3	Usually 4	Almost Always 5	Always 6

Questions

10. Does this child seem to do the behavior (to upset or annoy you) when you are trying to get him/her to do what you ask?

11. Does this child seem to do the behavior (to upset or annoy you) when you are not paying attention to him/her? (For example, if you are sitting on the opposite side of the room, interacting with another person.)

12. Does the behavior stop occurring shortly after you give this child the toy, food, or activity he/she has requested?

13. When the behavior is occurring, does the child seem calm, content, and unaware of anything else going on around him/her?

14. Does the behavior stop occurring shortly after (one to five minutes) you stop requesting or prompting this child to do things (e.g., clean up toys, engage in a difficult task, etc.)?

15. Does the behavior stop or not occur when the child has your full attention?

16. Does the behavior seem to occur when this child has been told he/she can't do something he/she had wanted to do?

Answers

Never 0	Almost Never 1	Seldom 2	Half the Time 3	Usually 4	Almost Always 5	Always 6

Never 0	Almost Never 1	Seldom 2	Half the Time 3	Usually 4	Almost Always 5	Always 6

Never 0	Almost Never 1	Seldom 2	Half the Time 3	Usually 4	Almost Always 5	Always 6

Never 0	Almost Never 1	Seldom 2	Half the Time 3	Usually 4	Almost Always 5	Always 6

Never 0	Almost Never 1	Seldom 2	Half the Time 3	Usually 4	Almost Always 5	Always 6

Never 0	Almost Never 1	Seldom 2	Half the Time 3	Usually 4	Almost Always 5	Always 6

Never 0	Almost Never 1	Seldom 2	Half the Time 3	Usually 4	Almost Always 5	Always 6

Sensory	Escape	Attention	Tangible
1. _____	2. _____	3. _____	4. _____
5. _____	6. _____	7. _____	8. _____
9. _____	10. _____	11. _____	12. _____
13. _____	14. _____	15. _____	16. _____
Total Score _____	_____	_____	_____

Adapted from Durand, V. M. (1988). *The Motivation Assessment Scale.* In M. Hersen & A. Bellack (Eds.), Dictionary of behavioral assessment techniques (pp. 309–310). Elmsford, NY: Pergamon.

APPENDIX B.

ABC Analysis (Blank Form)

Date Time	Antecedent	Behavior	Consequence	Possible Function

CHAPTER 5

Tools for the Toolbox: Strategies to Meet Challenging Behaviors

Deborah Hewitt & Cindy Croft

Setting the Stage

PHYSICAL, social, and emotional development have an impact on a child's understanding of their behavior and the behaviors of others around them. Children are constantly growing, learning, and discovering. From infancy and well into school age, children continue to grow physically, socially, and emotionally. This development influences their relationships, their view of themselves, and their eventual success in adulthood.

Physical development is a long continuum of growth and mastery of skills. A very young child might not have the physical size to reach a certain object and could cry loudly to gain attention to his dilemma. Another child might be physically larger than a peer and able to knock the other child over to reach a desired toy. Some children with physical disabilities might become frustrated if their environment is not adapted to meet their needs and throw a tantrum in that frustration. In order to enhance development and avoid some challenging behaviors, an early childhood program must examine each child's physical development and determine how to best meet that child's unique learning needs.

Social cognition is another key feature in children's behavior. Children give meaning to their social world early on. As they begin to interpret their experiences, they begin to see themselves as individuals and as a part of a larger community. An important role of the practitioner is to guide the social growth of children by introducing, enhancing, and expanding social skills. Gartrell (1998) speaks to mistaken behavior rather than misbehavior since it is through experiences that a child learns when it is okay and not okay to laugh loudly, to run inside, or to knock over someone else's tower of blocks. An early childhood program can effectively teach developmentally appropriate social skills that could prevent some challenging behaviors from occurring. When a behavior occurs that is not in keeping with a program's values, the teaching continues as the practitioner introduces a more appropriate behavioral response to the child.

According to Berk (1997), emotional development can be seen as a major force in "all aspects of human activity—cognitive, processing, social behavior and even physical health." As stated in earlier chapters, emotional development is a key component in a child's behavior and social skill acquisition. Emotional development occurs in a sequential manner as children master skills and move on to the next emotional milestone (Greenspan, 2002). Children who do not master skills such as emotional regulation will find it difficult to make and keep friends. Self-control is key to many childhood behaviors. If a child wants a particular object and has not yet developed a measure of self-control, he could use aggression to obtain the object. Early on, the toddler who bites or hits will find himself avoided by most of the other toddlers who may have been on the receiving end of the aggression. This social

isolation can inhibit other friendship skills such as cooperation and empathy (Croft, 2007).

Temperament also plays a key role in children's behavior (see chapter three). For example, a child with high intensity will display more emotion in their language, play, and social interactions that can sometimes lead to conflict or aggression. A child who is shy and more withdrawn could find it difficult to enter into play groups and hence may engage in more solitary play. A child with more fearfulness may resist changes in activities or environment. Berk (1997) asserts, "Since temperament represents an individual's emotional style, it should predict behaviors that emotions organize and regulate." Therefore, how an early childhood program responds to individual temperament styles can have a great impact on the behavior of children in that program. The process referred to as "goodness of fit" describes how temperament and environment can work together toward favorable outcomes for children (Croft, 2007).

A child's physical abilities, social skills, emotional development, and temperament must be considered as a practitioner develops strategies for working with a child who displays challenging behaviors. A combination of strategies designed to meet the needs of an individual helps increase a child's success in the early childhood program.

Specific Strategies for Meeting the Functional Needs of a Child's Behavior

As explained in the previous chapter, the function of any behavior is the need for a child to "get" or "get away from" an object, activity, attention, or sensation. In addition, children may engage in challenging behaviors because the behaviors are "working" for them and have meaning for them (CSEFEL, 2003). Once a practitioner has identified the function, she can go on to meet the child's need by adapting or changing the environment or practices. What follows in this chapter are specific strategies that can be employed by early childhood or school age practitioners in each of the functional areas as they relate to programming.

Objects
Objects are described as the components of the setting that can be touched, felt, or seen by children. Many challenging behaviors can oc-

cur because two children desire the same object (e.g., toy). Teaching children the skills they need to share a limited number of materials in an early childhood setting requires patience, creativity, and endurance. Children need time to learn ways to get their needs met in socially acceptable ways. Some children learn by watching others and some through the coaching of those around them. Other children need more specific instruction. Stories, puppet plays, and role plays can help all children learn the skills needed to control their impulses, take turns, and work out conflicts. If a child has learned to get what he wants in ways that are challenging to adults, it takes more time, planning, and strong teaching skills to help the child relearn more acceptable ways to meet his needs.

A child needs many social skills to learn how to interact with his peers. This requires that he coordinate his behavior with theirs and successfully obtains materials he wants to use in play. Suggestions for arranging the environment and ways to teach impulse control, turn taking, and problem solving follow. These are intended as examples upon which to build effective practices.

Environment. Careful consideration of the environment can help set the stage for success. Sometimes the goal of challenging behavior is to obtain a desired object. Make it easier for children to see and to access materials they want by arranging the environment in ways that allow them to be as independent as possible. Practitioners can also avoid or reduce the number of challenging behaviors by adding objects, removing objects, or arranging them in ways that support appropriate behavior. A few suggestions are listed here. For a more thorough description of the effects of the environment, see chapter two.

- ▶ Place toys and materials on low shelves and hooks so the children can help themselves as well as independently return materials to their places.
- ▶ Arrange materials in a way that children can easily see the selections and make decisions about what to play with. For example, display books on the bookshelf with the titles and covers facing forward. This way the child doesn't have to dig through a box or become frustrated looking through the books on a shelf before finding the one he wants.

▶ Label containers for materials with a picture and put the same picture on the shelf where the container is to be stored.

▶ Provide duplicates of favorite toys and desired or novel materials.

▶ Place some materials that are available for use on a table or on the floor. This might draw children to the area and encourage the type of play that is to take place. For instance, place a few puzzles out on the puzzle table rather than leaving them in the rack.

▶ Limit the number of children who can play in a popular area so there is less competition over desired toys. Place four water shirts near the water table to indicate four children can use these materials at one time. Or arrange two chairs at the computer station to show that two children can use the computer at once. This also encourages children to practice wait skills which supports self-regulation.

▶ Show where certain materials are to be used. For example, lay a hulahoop on the floor to indicate to the children where to stay with a punch ball.

▶ Use physical boundaries with shelving, furniture, and tape. Boundaries help children understand where different activities take place and also encourage their development of self-regulatory behaviors.

Impulse Control. Children learn through developmental stages to control their impulses to grab or take an object that another child might be using. A two-year-old will be less skilled than a four-year-old at waiting and sharing based on their emotional trajectory. Learning impulse control can also help children stop before hurting another child when they are angry. Teaching children to control their impulses can be difficult. One curriculum called Second Step: A Violence-Prevention Curriculum uses a puppet named Impulsive Puppy to introduce this concept (Committee for Children, 1991). It helps children recognize that like children, Impulsive Puppy sometimes does the first thing that pops into his head. It also helps children examine the consequences of impulsive behaviors and teaches them to think before acting. Children need many opportunities to learn to stop and control their impulses that help them learn to calm down when upset. These opportunities are present many times during the child care day through wait times, sharing opportunities, dramatic play, and book reading. The following are some specific examples.

Help children learn to stop their actions through a variety of strategies. Play movement games like "Red Light, Green Light" or moving to music and freezing when it stops. Provide a visual cue by using sign language along with words when you say stop. Or make a picture of a stop sign and place it on stick or heavy tag board to hold up when a child needs a visual reminder.

Help children recognize the physical signs that they are becoming upset. Do a role play in which you describe a situation when you were upset with yourself. For instance, talk about a time when you lost your keys and you looked and looked but couldn't find them. Show the children what you looked like when you were mad. Describe how your eyebrows went down, your hands were clenched, your tummy was tight, and you stomped your foot. Ask the children to show what they look like when they are mad. Draw simple pictures of the way they look or the things they describe. Tell the children that when a person feels angry it helps to calm down. Ask them to think about things they could do to calm down. They might take deep breaths, count to three, take a break at the sensory table, squeeze some play dough, or tell a grown up. Again draw or find simple pictures for each idea. Post them in your setting as a visual reminder. Repeat the role play using different situations like trying to fix something that isn't working or arguing about whose turn it was to get snack ready.

Help children recognize that they are upset by describing what you see. You might say, "You look mad. I see your eyebrows are down and your fists are tight." Or "I can see you are really excited. You are bouncing up and down and talking really fast." Remind them they need to calm down. Help them choose from the picture list what they would like to do to calm down. Increasing a child's emotional literacy by helping them find words for their feelings will also help them increase their ability to regulate their feelings and impulses (Croft, 2007).

Relaxation techniques can also be helpful to children who are distraught about an object they want. Keep in mind that slow and repetitive movements tend to be relaxing while fast, jerky ones are more stimulating (Cherry, 1981). Sometimes a child does well to sit, cuddled in an adult's lap while settling down. Use a secure but gentle cuddle and talk about how their engine is revved up or their breathing is fast and they need to slow down. Be sure to remain calm. Often the child will begin to match his breathing to that of the adult. Some children will not want to be touched. If this is the case, one of the following suggestions might be helpful.

▶ Show how a rag doll doesn't have any bones that help her stay up. Show the children how her hand flops to her side whenever it is held up. Pretend to be a rag doll. Raise one hand to shoulder height and let it drop, repeat with the other hand. Let your head drop to your chest. Drop from your waist with your hands hanging to the floor. Repeat each part two or three times (Cherry, 1981).
▶ Show the children how to take slow deep breaths to blow up a balloon. Let the balloon go, showing how it falls to the ground. Then act it out. Start by curling up in a ball on the floor. Pretend to grow a little with each deep breath. Finally, ask the children to float gently back into their position on the floor.
▶ Play soft calming music. Sit on the floor. Ask the children to place their hands on their knees. Have the children take slow deep breaths in through their nose and out through their mouth. Instruct them to make different sounds each time they exhale like "sh, ssss, or hee." Encourage them to try it with their eyes open, then with their eyes closed.
▶ Guide the children through a pretend scenario. Act out the following story or one that is similar to it. The kitten is playing with a ball of yarn. It is very excited but now it is time for the kitten to take a nap. The kitten goes to get a drink of milk. It turns around three times before it curls up on a pillow and closes its eyes. (Count to ten or more while the kitten is sleeping.) When the kitten wakes up, it yawns and stretches. Then it stands up and is ready to move slowly and quietly to the next activity.

Turn Taking. Infants begin to learn about turn taking through interactions with adults. As an infant and caregiver "converse" with each other, the baby coos and murmurs and the adult responds. When this pattern is repeated, a back and forth rhythm develops. Later as the child and caregiver play a game like "so big," the child learns to take turns during this simple interaction. From these modest beginnings, turn taking grows.

When two infants begin to interact with one another, they might find that they both want the same toy. Typically, the problem that arises can be quickly satisfied by offering a duplicate toy or substituting something that is similar. Toddlers who want the same toy at the same time will do well with a similar solution or might be redirected to another exciting activity. Practitioners can also begin to set up simple back and forth interactions between toddlers with a ball, car, or talking on a toy telephone. Toddler interactions are likely to be brief but help the child begin to practice this important skill.

Preschool age children will need repeated practice with turn taking. They need support during an upset over a toy as well as skills taught during instructional times throughout the day. Puppet plays, role plays, and stories about how others take turns with objects can be helpful models from which children can learn.

There are usually signals that alert practitioners to the fact their support is needed. Voices rise, children tug at a common toy or object, or perhaps a child begins to cry. At other times a practitioner knows her group of children well enough to recognize that supervision will be important when certain materials are available. Coaching can help children through most difficulties. Begin by describing the situation. Say something like "I see you and Samantha both want the shovel." This gives the children an opportunity to describe what has taken place. Then ask, "What could you do to work this out?" The children might be able to come up with some solutions, especially if they have been introduced to ways to share at instructional times. If they are unable to think of ideas, provide two solutions from which to choose, "We could get another shovel or one could hold the bucket while the other fills it up." If the children are still unable to resolve the dispute the practitioner may need to offer the solution, "You use the shovel now and when you are done give it to Samantha." Help Samantha decide what to do until the shovel is available. Ask her to look around the room and find what she wants to play. Help her settle into the activity. Be sure to notice when the first child is done with the shovel and help him offer it to Samantha.

This kind of coaching is essential when children are first learning to take turns. They need to hear the words to use or have someone speak the words for them. With repeated coaching a child may recall some of the solutions suggested in conflict situations and begin to apply them on their own.

Children can learn about taking turns by watching puppet plays. Puppets can act out situations that are similar to those encountered by the children and show a variety of solutions. For example, show two puppets arguing or scuffling over a toy truck. Stop the play and describe the problem. Say something like, "The chick and the duck both want the truck. What could they do to work it out?" If the children suggest that they share, help them describe it by asking, "What would that look like?" Act it out with the puppets. Ask the children if there is another way to work it out. Describe what that would look like and act it out. To end the lesson summarize by saying something like, "Chick and Duck had a problem. They both wanted the truck. They thought of two ways to work it out. First they drove the truck back and forth to each other then Chick played with the truck while Duck waited for a turn." Repeat this type of puppet play periodically using a variety of props. The puppets could argue over a book, a ball, or blocks. Remember to offer a number of different solutions to problems such as taking turns, making a trade, telling a grown up, or walking away.

Problem Solving. Problem solving skills build on impulse control and calming down when upset. Once a child stops his behavior and calms down, he can begin to think about possible solutions. When problem solving a child can choose from ideas he generates or options presented by an adult. The child then tries the best idea. When children problem solve they take a break from activity and will often times need help to reengage. Many times the practitioner will need to provide support throughout all the steps in problem solving. Problem solving is a more sophisticated social/emotional skill for children and involves mastery in perspective-taking and affiliation competencies as well (Gonzalez-Mena, 2009).

Present the steps in problem solving during instructional time (see Chapter One). One helpful strategy is to use a picture of a semaphore to illustrate the steps. The red light indicates that there is a problem and the children need to stop. The yellow light helps them remember to calm down and think of ways to solve the problem. The green light reminds the children to "go" and try their best idea (Hewitt and Heidemann 1998). Post the semaphore in a prominent spot. Do puppet plays and role plays to show how this works. See an example of a puppet play in the sidebar on page 114.

Using different stories, puppet plays, and role plays help to reinforce concepts involved in problem solving but children are likely to

CHICK has three plastic airplanes. Duck has only one. Duck complains that this isn't fair but Chick doesn't give him anymore airplanes. Stop the play and point to the red light. Say something like, "Chick and Duck need to stop. They have a problem. Chick has more airplanes than Duck and Duck is mad." Then point to the yellow light. Remind them that this means they need to calm down and think about what they could do. Have Duck take three deep breaths. Then ask the children, "What could Chick and Duck do so they would both be happy?" Use the puppets to act out their ideas (e.g., one for Duck then one for Chick or get more airplanes). Summarize the play and then finish by acting out one of the solutions saying, "Chick and Duck chose to give two airplanes to Chick and two to Duck." ✣

need a practitioner's help when they are in the middle of an upset. Carry a pocket-sized version of a picture of the semaphore and the pictures that are posted that depict possible solutions. When children are having trouble use these pictures or the ones posted in the room and guide the children through the steps in problem solving. When these important skills are learned in the early years they lay the groundwork for successful peer interaction in years to come.

Activities

Activities are the events or programmatic parts of the early childhood or school age setting. Challenging behaviors might occur if a child does not want to participate in an activity (i.e., sitting in circle time) or if the child wants to stay in an activity after it has ended (i.e., playing outside). Seeking the function of the child's behavior was laid out in greater detail in chapter four.

Encouraging Participation in Activities. Some challenging behaviors may arise because a child is not involved in activities with the rest of the children. A child who is used to playing alone may resent others who want to play near him and may see their involvement in the same area as an intrusion. Solitary play can be seen in children with some disabilities like autism or in children who not yet developed affiliation skills with others. Also, a child who has been left alone to play, perhaps because of previous behavior issues, may use the behavior to keep others at a safe distance. Aggression can result from one child who only wants to be left alone to play with the blocks, without interference from a playmate. Once another child enters the play area and begins to build along side him, he may strike out by hitting or knocking over the tower of blocks, thus sending the other child crying to the teacher. He will have met his goal of being left alone, at least for a while. A different child, also seeking to withdraw from activities, may refuse to join in with others, frustrating the practitioner who must now deal with the start of a new activity as well as a child whose behavior seems defiant.

Why do some children seem to prefer solitary play? There may be several factors that influence how well a child is engaged by the activities around him. Practitioners can avoid some behaviors by being observant of the child who seems to avoid activity and seeking to understand some key conditions. It is important that activities match the developmental levels of each child and the temperament needs of each child. In addition, giving options and choices can avoid a child's withdrawal from activities.

Match Developmental Level. Knowledge of child development is a key component to successfully matching program activities to each child's individual needs. There are broad categories of motor, cognition, and social developments that are comprised of typically achieved milestones. Careful observation of each child in an early childhood program will help the practitioner determine levels of development in order to make adaptations, when necessary, to activities for each child.

Challenging behaviors may arise when an activity is too hard or too easy for a child. A child can become frustrated if a task is too difficult, resulting in an angry response such as throwing the glue bottle to the floor, or yelling at his neighbor. Or he could refuse to do the task, knowing that he has had difficulty in the past with it. If a task is too easy, a practitioner could see behaviors such as a child interfering with others who haven't finished the project yet, or a child who leaves the area and begins running around the room. Several strategies can be applied to avoid challenging behaviors resulting from a child's developmental level not matching the task or activity at hand.

▶ Teach children about their feelings. Some children may not be at the same developmental stage emotionally as peers. Help children to identify, acknowledge, accept and then describe their feelings. This can be done with books, feelings flash cards, role play, dramatic play and modeling. By giving a child a feeling vocabulary, he has the tools he needs to express himself when he is frustrated or bored with a task or activity.

▶ Lessen the task demand if a child is easily frustrated with it. Keep the task short, simple and well defined. Some children may benefit from activity cards that show them each step to follow.

▶ Encourage collaboration activities by giving visual and verbal attention to cooperation between children. Help children learn to help each other.

▶ Provide a range of developmental levels in toys and activities.

Meet Temperament Needs. A child's temperament has much to do with how he will react to the world around him (see Chapter Three). Children who are shy or withdrawn may find it difficult to become involved in activities with other children without some prompting or verbal cues from an adult. Some children may need some time away from a group activity in order to calm themselves or take a break from sensory stimulation. Help a child learn a process to teach themselves how to recognize and regulate their own need for time away. Give them tools to accomplish this in a calm, organized way.

▶ Create a "feelings cube" for children to use during the day to express if they are feeling shy or quiet, and need some time alone.
▶ Develop a signal for a child that he can use to say, "I need to take a break." Children can lose control of their emotions in certain situations and need to learn to recognize the signs leading up to that point in their own bodies. In the beginning, the practitioner may be the one who tells a child, "You're pretty upset at Evan, you need to take a deep breath, and then we'll talk." Eventually, the child will be empowered to initiate the break for himself. Use a tangible signal that the child can easily recognize, like using your hand as a stop signal.
▶ Avoid power struggles by finding a way to say "yes."
▶ Let a child who has a low sensory threshold withdraw to a quiet area occasionally. Allow a child who is more introverted to say he wants to play alone for a while.
▶ Give children exercises for calming themselves like taking deep breathes or closing their eyes and relaxing their body. Help them know they can use these calming practices when they feel their "engines" revving up.

Give Options and Choices. Children may be reluctant to join others in play based on limited preferences for activities or toys. On the other hand, all the different play areas available to them in free play or the drama center might overwhelm another child. Giving children options and helping them learn to make choices is part of the practitioner's role in promoting emotional and social development. A practitioner must also recognize when children need extra help in making choices or when they need fewer options in order to make a choice. The following are some strategies for helping children build skills around making choices in order to become more active in their participation with others.

▶ Help a child try something new. Use a high probability sequence: identify something the child really likes to do, and then request a follow through with something he isn't as likely to try. Continue to link preferred tasks to less frequently tried activities.

▶ Limit choices for some children who have difficulty choosing or difficulty moving on to another activity. Also, for children who seem unable to choose, look closely at your environment. Look for clutter, which can keep a child confused and unable to make a choice. Look for ways to lessen clutter; for example, store like items together, keep things in a consistent place, clearly label items, space items so they are not so close to each other.

▶ Some children may need different options in order to participate with others. If some events are known to be problematic for the child, allow for an alternative. For instance, if a child avoids physical activity because he feels uncoordinated, guide him to activities that he can excel at and will build on his gross motor skills.

▶ Outline the choices clearly so the child understands what they are. Give him time to make a good choice, and then affirm his ability to make a good choice.

▶ For the child who is seeking to "get away" from an object, activity, attention, or sensation, reducing distractions or competing events, materials, etc. may help keep him engaged. For the child who is trying to "get" or obtain something, choices in the child's interest may distract him when access cannot be provided (CSEFEL, 2003).

▶ Choices can be offered using photographs, visuals, or actual objects. (CSEFEL, 2003).

Teaching Skills and Mastery of Skills. A challenging behavior can occur because a child is frustrated with the difficulty of a task. As stated earlier, knowing the developmental level of each child in a program will help the practitioner better gauge when and how to introduce new activities or tasks. Combining these strategies will help you give children the skills to enter in and out of play and activities as they grow socially and emotionally.

▶ Give a child opportunities to frequently repeat a task or activity until they have achieved mastery of it. Frequent repetition helps the child learn as well as develop self-esteem.

▶ Clearly define interest areas so children know what is expected in that area, or what they will be doing in order to feel successful.

▶ Break a task into several steps so a child can experience success at each interval. The activity will seem less overwhelming if it is in smaller parts.

Helping Children Transition To or From Activities. Another common area for challenging behaviors to occur is during the movement between activities or program events. Some children have great difficulty making changes. Behaviors such as refusing to leave an area, noncompliance, tantruming, and aggression might result from a child who is not equipped emotionally to move comfortably from event to event. Several strategies can be used to reduce the stress level of the child and subsequent behavior challenges that might result from transitions.

Program Approaches to Changes. All children at some point will prefer not to leave a play area or a preferred activity. Practitioners can help children by examining their own program schedules carefully and implementing changes where needed. Avoiding a challenging behavior by adapting the need for movement within a program is key. Also, teaching some specific skills for transitions to children will be a useful tool for preventing some problems during change times. Some program changes include:

▶ Reduce the overall number of transitions each day.
▶ Plan ahead by letting children know when there will be changes to the regular schedule. Also, within the regular schedule, give five-minute warnings to prepare for ending the activity. Some children may need multiple cues in order to ready themselves for a change. Use visual prompts like TimeTimer® to help children see that a change is coming.
▶ Give some children extra time that may need it.
▶ Allow materials to go from one area to another, when possible.
▶ Reduce the chaos of some transitions, by sending one child at a time. For example, if the children are transitioning from group time to washing hands, give each child an opportunity to answer a question or do a short activity before going to the sink. The group might all be monkeys jumping on the bed, but one is dismissed to the sink when her name is placed in the phrase, "Jenna fell off and bumped her head." Or the group can sing, "The bear went over

the mountain," then dismiss one at time by singing, "Vincent went over the mountain."

▶ Use a picture schedule that helps build a sense of safety and security for children. Activity schedules are also useful for some children who may need to know what happens within a specific activity.

Some specific strategies that help children learn to wait or help them increase their ability to transition include:

▶ Use an activity book to describe the sequence of actions for a given event. The pages of the book might contain pictures for each step, laminated so it can be used again.

▶ Keep a bag of open ended waiting gadgets handy for especially difficult transitions. Party favors such as mini Slinkys, kaleidoscopes, pinwheels, or squeeze balls are inexpensive gadgets that can be passed out, used while waiting, and then collected until next time they are needed.

▶ Capture the interest of the group with an "attention getter." While the children finish an activity and begin to settle into the next, pique their curiosity about what is to come. Introduce the new activity by wearing a costume, showing a prop, giving clues about the next activity, or asking questions that they can answer at the end of the game or story.

▶ Give choices to children who have difficulty with the clean up transition. Encourage participation by letting the child choose if he will clean the blocks or the puzzles. Another choice might be to decide if he will pick up the blocks while you place them in the shelf or the other way around, where you bring him the blocks and he places them where they go.

▶ Post a photo in each area of the room that provides an example of what it is to look like when it is clean.

▶ Use a picture schedule to help children understand what is happening now and what is going to happen next. Make a picture schedule for the day or even for specific activities, like a field trip. Specify each step of the schedule in an easy to understand format. By teaching children to use a picture or activity schedule, we give them predictability, security, confidence, and independence.

Routines. Children learn better when they have a consistent routine that is predictable. A chaotic, unpredictable schedule may increase a child's anxiety level, which in turn may increase a child's "acting out" behaviors (Klein, Cook, and Richardson-Gibbs, 2001). Routines help children in their development of self-regulation skills.

▶ Provide a consistent daily schedule that is also flexible.

▶ Be consistent so a child knows what to expect. Help him feel safe using the same words, same routine, etc. for each activity of the day.

▶ Tell children that the toys will be in the same place tomorrow when they come back as they are today; positive "teacher talk" helps build a child's sense of safety and security as they build a relationship with you. This is particularly important for children who may be experiencing stress or anxiousness.

▶ Practice and fine-tune skills that are part of the daily routine that may be difficult for a child who is challenged by transitions. For instance, if a child does not move well from the play area to the lunchroom, help him learn to master the skills of putting away toys and then getting his lunch sack at a time other than the actual transition. Some routines may be easier than others to master, depending on the child's special need. Be open to cues the child gives about difficulty of a particular routine, and think of creative ways for him to master it.

Attention
Attention refers to the child obtaining recognition by the practitioner or a peer. Challenging behavior can occur when a child wants attention that he is not getting or when he wants to avoid the attention he receives. For instance, a child might be overly loud in order to gain attention from his teacher or might become embarrassed and begin to cry if he is not comfortable being "star" of the day.

Children differ in their need for attention. Some seem to be insatiable while others ask for so little attention practitioners need to make a point of interacting with the child. A child who seems insatiable may require what seems like constant attention to stay on task or remain appropriate. This child might call your name many times per hour, ask to have you look at and approve of things he makes, try to help when

help isn't needed, or talk when you are talking. Another child might not make a point of obtaining your attention for days at a time.

Just as children require different amounts of attention children also respond individually to different types of attention. Some are highly motivated to receive the attention of the group, others become embarrassed when they are singled out. Practitioners need to tune in to the type of attention that is comfortable to each individual in their group and match their own behavior to the needs of the child.

Giving Different Types of Attention. Attention can take many forms. It can range from spending one-on-one time with an adult to receiving the thumbs up signal from across the room. Adult attention might consist of:

► Holding hands while walking down the hall
► Playing a clapping game like "peas porridge hot"
► Cuddling
► Reading a story together
► Telling the child you appreciate his help

Time spent together can be short. Make sure the attention is given at a time when the child is behaving appropriately. Try to meet his need for attention by spending time early in the day and often. This way the child may not need to engage in challenging behavior in order to gain attention. Develop a positive relationship with each child by attending to and entering into play with him. Follow the child's lead in play to give the child an opportunity to control play situations and build self-esteem. Greenspan's method of interaction is called "Floor Time." This one-on-one playtime helps practitioners provide positive attention by relating to the child in a warm, personal way (Greenspan, 2002). For a thorough discussion of this technique and its benefits see chapter three.

A child who is shy might respond to nonverbal attention. Nonverbal attention can also help to acknowledge or remain in contact with a child whose need for attention is high. Nonverbal attention might include:

- ▶ Thumbs up signal
- ▶ Okay signal
- ▶ Wink
- ▶ Nod
- ▶ Smile
- ▶ Special signal developed between the adult and the child
- ▶ Pat on the back

Asks for Attention in Appropriate Ways. One of the things that a child who seeks attention may need to learn is to ask for attention in appropriate ways. Teach a child to say the name of the person from whom he wants attention or pat her arm. Help him learn to wait for that person to look at him before making his request. Give him the words to use to ask for help or ask someone to join him. Keep in mind that challenging behavior can sometimes mean that this child needs time with an adult. Help him learn to use words to ask for this so challenging behavior can be avoided. If the child forgets to move close to the adult and ask for attention, interpret his behavior for him saying something like, "Oh Charlie, did you want my attention? You could pat my arm and say, 'Claire.' Then I'll look at you and you can tell me what you want."

Teach the child to obtain the attention of his peers in the same way. For instance, if Troy tries to tell Jacob that he wants some of the blocks, but Jacob doesn't respond, Troy might become frustrated and start yelling or crying. Teach Troy to touch Jacob's arm or say his name. Wait until Jacob looks at him and then say in a big, strong voice, "I need some blocks, too." The practitioner may need to coach Jacob to look at Troy. Then work through the steps in problem solving with both children. With help, Troy can learn an alternative to crying in order to get Jacob's attention.

Make Attention Contingent on Appropriate Behavior. When children strive to obtain adult attention, it is important to attend when the child is behaving appropriately. For example, a child might delay getting his coat on in an effort to get attention. Make it clear to this child that after he gets his coat on there will be a short time to spend together before the bus comes. When it is necessary to intervene with a child who is using a challenging behavior to seek attention, try to keep the interaction simple with little "payoff" for the child. Later, when the child is using behaviors that you want to encourage, give full attention to him with much energy and animation.

Entering a Group. Children try many different techniques to obtain the attention of peers and join their play. Some strategies are more successful than others. Some children enter play in a way that is disruptive to the ongoing play. When children do this it is understandable that the group rejects this type of intrusion and finds it difficult to adjust their play to include this child. A child who approaches two or three other children who are building a tower is likely to be met with protests if he says, "I want this block over here," and then moves things they have already arranged.

Children reject the attempts of others for a number of reasons. They may say that another child can't play because they are trying to protect a limited number of toys and materials. For instance, three children might each have three toy cars. If another were to approach, they may not want to divide the toys further. Children might be trying to protect the roles they have established. If a group of children are playing restaurant, they may have already decided who is pretending to be the server, the customer, and the cook. If an additional child comes, they may not understand how to expand their play to include another

role like the cashier or the delivery person. Sometimes children reject others based on past experience with an individual. For example, if the child has been aggressive in the past they may remember the behavior and refuse to play with him.

Practitioners can help children learn to approach existing play in a way that helps them gain the attention of others and successfully enter the group. One way is to have the child observe the play for a short time. Talk with the child about what is taking place and how he could be part of it. Help the child consider a new role and what actions that person (or animal) would take. For example, if there is a group of children playing house, one is the mother and the other the big sister, the newcomer might be the babysitter. He can knock on the door and say, "Hi, I'm the babysitter." Help give this child the words to use and ideas about things he can do in this role before he actually approaches play.

Another successful strategy is for the newcomer to offer a prop related to the existing play. Children who are playing Pizza Hut® may welcome someone who brings money that they have made in the writing center to share with the customers. Or if the newcomer can offer just the right block to stabilize a building, his chances of being welcomed are much greater.

A child who has a reputation of being aggressive will need an adult to reassure the other children that he is learning to play without hurting others. Say something like, "Jeremy really likes to play with the trucks too. He's learning to use words. I'll be right here to help things go smoothly." Sometimes the reputation can outlive the behavior and an adult needs to help the children recognize that the child has many strengths. Point out the child's abilities by saying something like, "Leachia is really good at puzzles. Remember the other day when she helped you with the lion puzzle? She can help you with this one too." Our goal is to help all children develop social competencies through interactions with peers. We want every child to learn to communicate his needs effectively.

Sometimes a newcomer is more likely to be accepted when he joins the group without conversation. Encourage the child to sit next to the others and do the same thing. For instance, a child can join others in the housekeeping area just by walking in and starting to stir a pot. Or if a child wants to join others in the sandbox, provide him with a shovel and bucket, and clear a spot for him to sit. Requiring that children ask to play is oftentimes ineffective.

Second Step® suggests that children learn to compliment the play of others as an opening line. Teach a child to use a phrase that begins with, "I like _____." He can fill in the blank with any appropriate compliment such as "the tower you're making." Then have the child declare that he likes to build or draw too. With that said, the newcomer can sit down and get started (Second Step, 1991).

Sensations

Sensations encompass a child's sensory intake including sight, smell, hearing, taste, as well as the tactile, vestibular, and proprioceptive senses. Children may be over stimulated in one or more senses; for instance, a child can react to lots of noise and strike out at another child. In the same way, children can be underresponsive in their sensory systems. A child who is understimulated in his gross muscle system might hug other children too tightly or run into the teacher to get a hug. Children with sensory processing difficulties may use behaviors to avoid or obtain sensory input. Practitioners need to use a keen eye to discover the function for any child's challenging behavior to see if there is a sensory link.

Helping Children who are Seeking Sensory Stimulation. One of the nine basic temperament traits is sensory awareness. Children may be high, low, or somewhere in between in their need for sensory stimulation or feedback. Kranowitz (1998) refers to the out-of-sync child, meaning the child whose reactions to the world around him are out of the norm, high or low, compared to his peers. A temperament sorter might rate how sensitive a child is in each of his sensory channels, which include pain, touch, taste, smell, hearing, and sight. When trying to determine a child's sensory threshold, a practitioner would look to clues such as how aware a child seems to be of noises, changes in temperature or lighting, smells, textures. When looking at a child who may need more sensory stimulation in one or more areas, a practitioner could see behaviors that help the child get to that sensory need. A practitioner might avoid some challenging behaviors from a child if she helps the child meet his sensory need in more constructive ways.

Encourage Diverse Sensory Experiences. A quality early childhood program will include multi-sensory experiences for all young children. For the child who requires more sensory feedback, building on what is already part of the program is important. This can be accomplished in many ways. For instance, give children the opportunity for motor exploration using water play (Klein, Cook, and Richardson-Gibbs, 2001). Water play can be expanded when weather permits, by moving it outside for greater splashing and sloshing. A sand table allows for greater sensory stimulation to children and can incorporate many other mediums as well. Expanding on play with sand could include introducing other textures within the sand: adding water, mixing other ingredients with sand at another table, using different types of sand, finer and courser. Art activities open up an endless supply of sensory experiences: glue, watercolor, finger paint, collages, etc. all let a child touch and feel various textures. Allow a child who likes to touch things to have a "sensory bag" nearby with Koosh balls, gloop, Silly Putty, etc. The dramatic play center is an area that can include many textures and objects that encourage rich sensory experiences. Books can be purchased or made from scratch that include "touch and feel" pages. Encouraging diverse sensory experiences is as broad as a practitioner's imagination!

Adapting the Setting for Children Who Need a Break from Stimulation. Just as some children need to have more stimulation, there are children whose sensory processing needs make it more difficult to adjust to lots of sensory experiences. Again, there can be many variables in which senses are affected. A child might only react to one sense, such as bright light, or they may have a combination of sensory sensitivities such as noise and odors. A practitioner, who observes certain challenging behaviors at certain times of the day or in areas of the program, might begin to see a pattern in the child of over-awareness of one or more of his senses. Giving the child the opportunity to choose a different setting, if possible (leaving the noisier play area for a reading corner), or choosing a more preferable activity (painting with brushes instead of fingers) could avoid the need from the child to "get away" from something unpleasant. It takes awareness and keen observation from the practitioner to be in tune to a child who is sensory overstimulated.

Environment Changes and Adaptations. Making changes to the environment to lessen sensory stimulation can often be readily done. Take time to examine your environment for sounds, visual effects, smells, and textures that make up a child's daily experiences. What can be feasibly altered? Do you have an area than can be transformed into a more sterile space for a child to go to when he needs a break? Look for other changes that can be made such as:

- Diffuse sounds by using rugs, acoustic tile, fabric, or artwork hung on the walls (Klein, Cook and Richardson-Gibbs, 2001).
- Lessen visual distraction by fastening down banners, posters, signage, etc. that may move with the wind or motion in the room.
- Simplify what is hanging on the walls and ceiling.
- Cover a shelf of toys with a sheet when it is not in use.
- Lessen the noise distractions in the environment. Look for fluorescent lights that may need changing because of flickering. There are

diffusers that can be hung over fluorescent lights which soften the light.

▶ Take time to stop and listen to your program: are there many adults talking, a loud fan, lots of background noises? Do you have headphones available at times?

▶ Does your food area have a lot of strong smells during lunch preparation? Look for ways to keep the odors in one area if possible.

For a child who is feeling overstimulated in an early childhood program, being given many choices at once may be too much to process. Learn to slow down when possible. Take time to offer a variety of sensory experiences one at a time rather than all at once.

Creating a Quiet Space. Sometimes the simplest strategy for avoiding a challenging behavior that may come from sensory overload is to have a place where each child knows they can go to in order to "get away" from the distractions. This can be a corner of the room that is marked off, the reading or library area, or a collection of large beanbags for older children. Other ways you can create quiet space include:

▶ Divide up your area to allow children private time, paired activities, or small and large group activities.

▶ Provide space for children to go to if they want to be alone. Keep this space free from distractions by keeping displayed material and activity choices to a minimum. Be sure this space is in plain view so it can be supervised.

▶ Place activities that are generally quieter, next to one another.

▶ Place a rocking chair in quiet corner.

▶ Add a sensory activity like water play or play dough to your quiet space to soothe a child who is overstimulated.

▶ Let children know they can take a break when they need to so they learn to regulate themselves.

Always remember to respect a child's needs. Some children are easygoing by temperament, and will flow from activity to activity, sensory experience to sensory experience, with little effect most of the time. All children will become tired at times, have a "tough" day for some reason, and may need more careful regard to their sensory needs.

Some children will be under or overstimulated by their environment and need their practitioner to be alert to changes in their behavior throughout each day. Being aware of a child's specific temperament needs will help the practitioner avoid behaviors that are triggered by a child's desire to "get" or "get away" from sensory experience.

Summary

In chapter four, the function of behavior is explained in great detail. Simply put, challenging behaviors can be motivated by a desire to "get" or "get away from" an object, activity, attention, or sensations. After taking time to discover the function of the specific challenging behavior, practitioners will need to choose strategies that help a child learn to meet his needs in more acceptable ways. This supports his social and emotional development as well.

Each practitioner comes with her own "toolbox" of strategies she has developed from experience. The strategies found in this chapter are provided as additional "tools" for the practitioner to employ. By making use of a variety of tools, the practitioner can help children who demonstrate challenging behaviors be successful in the early childhood setting. The environment can be adapted to meet the needs of a child who may need more or less stimulation or may need help in accessing materials. Children can be helped to learn to control their impulses through movement games and relaxation techniques. Stories, puppet plays, and coaching can help teach turn taking and problem solving. Activities can be adapted so children become full participants and choices can be offered for those individuals who occasionally need a break from activity. Changes from one activity to another can be easier for children when practitioners reduce the number of transitions and carefully plan activities that help to reduce waiting time. Children who use challenging behavior to gain the attention of adults or their peers can learn to ask for attention in appropriate ways. Children can be recognized in ways that do not cause embarrassment or unwanted attention. Children can be taught to enter the play of others in ways that increase the likelihood of their being accepted.

Occasionally, a child will need services that are outside the parameters of an early childhood program. In that case, the practitioner would help the parent find resources for contacting their local early intervention services or local school district special education or county mental health services. Parents would then begin a more formal referral process for specific services to their child.

KEY POINTS

1. The physical, social, and emotional development of young children will impact their behaviors at different times in different ways.

2. Early childhood practitioners are in a unique position to view a child's behavior in the context of their whole development and make adjustments or adaptations in programming to meet the developmental needs of each child.

3. The function of a child's behavior will point practitioners to strategies that can be put into place to avoid or change challenging behaviors.

4. Practitioners can help children learn to "get" or "get away from" objects by teaching them to control impulses, take turns, and problem-solve.

5. Practitioners encourage appropriate participation in activities by taking time to match the developmental level of the activity to the individual, meeting a child's need to take a break, and by providing activity choices.

6. Children feel a sense of security when routines are consistent and predictable. Children who have difficulty changing from one activity to another can learn to cope with transitions when the number of changes is limited, and those that take place are well planned.

7. Children differ in their need for attention as well as their desire for group or individual attention. Practitioners need to be aware of the types of attention and meet the needs of individuals. Care needs to be given to teach the child appropriate ways to obtain the attention of adults and peers.

8. Children can be over or understimulated by the information they receive through their senses and challenging behaviors can result. Practitioners need to offer diverse sensory experiences and adjust the environment to meet the needs of individuals.

9. A combination of strategies might be required before a practitioner sees an end to a challenging behavior.

REFERENCES

Allen, K. and Schwartz, I. (2001). *The Exceptional Child: Inclusion in Early Childhood Education.* Albany, NY: Thompson Learning.

Berk, L. (1997). *Child Development.* Needham, MA: Allyn & Bacon.

The Center on the Social and Emotional Foundations for Early Learning (CSEFEL). (2003). *Promoting Social Emotional Competence.* University of Illinois-Champaign: Child Care Bureau. Head Start Bureau.

Cherry, C. (1981). *Think of Something Quiet.* Belmont, CA: Pitman.

Committee for Children (1991). *Second Step: A Violence-Prevention Curriculum.* Seattle, WA: Committee for Children.

Croft, Cindy (2007). *The Six Keys: Strategies for Promoting Children's Mental Health in Early Childhood Programs.* Farmington, MN: Sparrow Media Group.

Gartrell, Dan (1998). *A Guidance Approach for the Encouraging Classroom.* Albany, NY: Delmar Publishers.

Gonzalez-Mena, J. (2009). *Child, Family, and Community: Family-Centered Early Care and Education.* Merrill: Pearson Education Inc.

The Greenspan Floor Model. (August 5, 2002). *Five Steps in Floor Time.* Available at http://www.coping.org/ earlyin/floortm.htm.

Hewitt, D. (1995). *So This is Normal Too? Teachers and Parents Working Out Developmental Issues in Young Children.* St. Paul: Redleaf Press.

Hewitt, D. and Heidemann, S. (1998). *The Optimistic Classroom. Creative Ways to Give Children Hope.* St. Paul: Redleaf Press.

Klein, D., Cook, R., and Richardson-Gibbs, A. (2001). *Strategies for Including Children with Special Needs in Early Childhood Settings.* Albany, NY: Thompson Learning.

Kranowitz, Carol. (1998). *The Out-of-Sync Child: Recognizing and Coping with Sensory Integration Dysfunction.* New York: Penguin Putnam Press

McDonald, J. and Gillette, Y. (1985). "Taking Turns: Teaching Communication to your Child," *The Exceptional Parent, 15,* 49–52.

PART 3

Including Children
with Specific
Behavioral Disabilities

CHAPTER 6

ADHD:
Seeing the Disability
Behind the Behavior

Dea Anderson & Colleen Pachel

Attention Deficit Hyperactive Disorder

ACTIVE, lively, energetic, and unrestrained are words that describe most young children. In an early childhood classroom, children often display these characteristics, which are considered to be typical, developmentally appropriate behaviors. Toddlers are expected to walk, run, and maintain constant motion during their waking hours. Toddlers generally do not sit still unless something of intense interest captures their attention. Even then, their attention tends to be brief and they quickly move on to explore their world. As toddlers enter the preschool years, they continue to be physically active. In general, the attention spans of preschoolers begin to lengthen and they can stay with an activity for longer periods of time. Preschoolers also begin to show signs of learning self-regulation or self-control. As children develop, they use self-control to focus their energy and attention, which enables them to continue learning about their world.

The basic principles of child development tell us that young children develop in a relatively orderly sequence. Although children develop at varying rates, their development usually proceeds in a predictable direction from simple-to-complex understandings and concrete-to-abstract thinking. Early childhood practitioners will, more likely than not, meet children who do not follow the predicted path of development. Some children may continue to display short attention spans, be more active than their peers, and have difficulty controlling their energy. Inattentive, excessively active, and impulsive are words often used to describe children that display these characteristics on a regular basis. These three characteristics are the core symptoms of Attention Deficit Hyperactive Disorder.

What is Attention Deficit Hyperactive Disorder?

Attention Deficit Hyperactive Disorder (ADHD) is a diagnosable, treatable, biologically based disorder. ADHD is sometimes referred to as Attention Deficit Disorder (ADD), but the current "official" medical diagnosis is Attention Deficit Hyperactive Disorder. In recent years ADHD has received much attention in the media, which has led to increased public awareness and interest in the disorder. This increased interest has resulted in research that has enabled professionals to learn a great deal about ADHD in the last twenty years. Currently, ADHD is one of the most frequent childhood disorders and a common reason children are referred to mental health professionals. According to a report released by the Centers for Disease Control, four and one-half million children (7%) ages 3 to 17 years had ADHD in 2006. ADHD begins in childhood and can last into an individual's adult life. Research indicates that about one-half to two-thirds of children with ADHD will continue to display symptoms throughout adulthood. The primary symptoms of ADHD are inattention, hyperactivity, and impulsivity. These symptoms often appear between the ages of four and six years, but can occur earlier.

Inattention, impulsivity, and hyperactivity are present in all children and adults to some degree at some particular time. The difference is that an individual with ADHD will exhibit these symptoms with increased frequency, intensity, and duration. The levels of the symptoms displayed are not age-appropriate and/or situation-appropriate. Since most healthy children exhibit varying degrees of these symptoms, it is imperative that early childhood and school age care professionals have a thorough understanding of child development. A clear sense of typical child development and experience observing and working with young children often places early childhood practitioners in a crucial role in indentifying young children who display symptoms of ADHD. Most children with ADHD do not exhibit all of

A PARENT of a child who had recently been diagnosed with ADHD began to feel that the numbers of children diagnosed with ADHD and on medication were getting out of control. She wondered, "Why are there so many more children today with it [ADHD]? When I was a child of the 50s, there weren't as many and families were even bigger then. What is different now?" She began to think of what life and daily routines were like for her as a child years ago. She came to a conclusion that can serve as food for thought. In her early years, typical daily chores required far more physical work, for instance doing the laundry. You had to fill the tub on the washer with water from a hose and a second tub for rinse. After the clothes had agitated, you had to dip your hand into the water, pull out the clothes and manually feed them through the wringer. They would fall into the rinse water and then you again would reach in and pull them out and feed them back through the wringer to squeeze out excess water. They fell into a basket. From there you carried the basket out to the clothesline and hung the clothes. In between batches, you would take down the dry clothes and carry them into the house. Standing at the ironing board or a table, you would sprinkle each item with water and roll them tight. You would place each into a basket, and then cover them with a towel where they would wait until you were ready to iron them. It was an all-day process and was very tiring. Children who were required to help with these chores had no time to sit idle. Their physical energy was spent and their minds were occupied. Today, laundry day is quite different. The clothes are thrown into an automatic washer and when they are done you throw them in the dryer and when the buzzer sounds, your chore is done. Not much for physical expenditure and lots of free time.

Many chores of early generations were that way. ADHD has been around for a long time—it was just not as evident. ‡

the symptoms of the disorder. Symptoms have been observed to be different between boys and girls. Boys are more likely to display hyperactivity. They tend to show more symptoms of increased physical activity and difficulty controlling their bodies. Girls tend to display symptoms of inattention and are often referred to as "daydreamers." Needless to say, it is not difficult to understand why two to three times more boys are diagnosed with ADHD than girls. This does not

SAM struggled through kindergarten and first grade. Thinking that he was not as mature as a majority of his peers, his parents had him repeat first grade. The struggles continued for him and his family tried to understand and help him through, but it seemed that one battle led to another. His parents tried to work with his teachers using a reward system. At the beginning of the week, Sam could choose a goal that he worked toward. It could be a special time with one of his parents, going to the movies or seeing a sports game—it was his choice. He would bring home a journal where he was to record his daily assignments. If he was able to complete all of the week's work, he would receive his reward Friday or over the weekend, depending on what his choice was for a reward. Monday would go okay, with enthusiasm running high. On Tuesday, his goal was still attainable, but by Wednesday, interest was low and he would express that he couldn't do it. By Thursday, he could no longer see himself reaching the goal at all and would give up. Friday brought frustration and anger, usually followed by extreme negative behavior. He felt that he was a failure, and these emotions were thrown into the mental file with so many others. What was discovered was that Sam needed to work toward short-term goals that he could clearly see happening. He experienced success if the time between the goal or task and the reward were close together. For instance, watching 15 minutes of TV followed working on his homework for 15 minutes. After he saw that he could reach his goal in a short amount of time, his self-esteem improved and success was felt. Eventually he could work toward somewhat longer periods of time. He needed to make the connection between the goal and the reward. ‡‡

necessarily mean that more boys have ADHD than girls. It does indicate that the behaviors associated with ADHD are often more conspicuous and disruptive in boys.

The degree to which ADHD affects children varies by individual and environment. Studies show that ADHD does not influence intelligence but can make life difficult for some children. Although many children with ADHD are very bright, they are often developmentally behind their peers in attention, learning, and self-control.

The intensity of the core symptoms of distractibility, hyperactivity, and impulsivity frequently affect children's functioning at home, preschool, in child care and school age care experiences, and in some social situations. Sometimes children's behaviors are so severe and pervasive that the result is a significant degree of impairment in their ability to function within various environments. This places children at risk for future academic failure and development of low self-esteem. Therefore, it is critical for early childhood and school age care practitioners to take a more in-depth look at the primary symptoms.

Inattention/Distractibility

Children who have symptoms of inattention may be easily distracted, miss details, forget things, and frequently switch from one activity to another. Moving from one activity to another can be the result of becoming bored with the activity after only a few minutes or because of difficulty with being able to focus on one thing. It is generally quite challenging for children who are challenged by distractibility to focus attention on organizing and completing a task. Children with symptoms of inattention and distractibility may be observed rushing from activity-to-activity and then found wandering around the surroundings because they don't know what to do next. Learning something new can be frustrating due to an impaired ability to sustain attention. A number of children with issues of inattention and distractibility "tune out" or seem to often be daydreaming. They appear to drift into their own thoughts and lose track of what is taking place around them. They may appear to become easily confused and move more slowly than other children. When children with inattention fail to follow a direction or respond to a question, it is not necessarily because they deliberately choose not to listen. The more likely reason is that they did not hear the direction or question. They may also have difficulty processing information as quickly and accurately as others. Although children with inattentive symptoms might not appear to be physically hyperactive, their heads are filled with racing thoughts and constant stimuli. They have a brain that is hyperactive. Some children are particularly sensitive to environmental stimuli such as sight, sound, and touch. Visual stimuli such as color and movement distract some children while others are distracted by auditory stimuli. Auditory stimuli include background noises and/or unusual sounds. Distractibility is not necessarily observed at all times. When receiving individual attention, many children with symptoms of inattention and distractibility can attend to an activity for an extended period of time. Distractibility is on occasion disguised because a child can stay with a particular activity for an unusually long period of time. This is referred to as the ability to "hyper-focus." Usually the activity is highly stimulating, of great interest to the child, and has given the child an opportunity to experience some level of success.

Hyperactivity

Children who display symptoms of hyperactivity are in constant motion or "always on the go." They have difficulty sitting still and can be observed wiggling, tapping fingers and toes, shaking a leg or foot, and fidgeting with an object or fidgeting with a friend. Most young children are physically active. What distinguishes a child with ADHD is not necessarily the level of activity but their inability to inhibit their movement. Some children can slow their bodies down upon request, but can only do so for a very short period of time. Many children with ADHD will become even more active when tired, hungry, anxious, or in an

DOUG, who is four years old and not yet diagnosed with ADHD, and his older brother and younger sister are told that they can put their shoes and jackets on for playing outside. Doug is still sitting with his shoe in hand when the other two children are headed out the door. His mom approaches Doug with a frustrated disposition and asks why it takes him so long to get ready. As the conversation escalates, Doug ends up crying, throwing his shoe, and yelling at mom. Mom reacts by telling Doug that he needs to stay inside. Doug goes crying and screaming to his room and mom leaves the battle feeling drained once again. ✄

unfamiliar situation. Children with symptoms of hyperactivity have a tendency to be restless sleepers, toss, turn, and call out in their sleep. The activity level of children with ADHD is typically not goal-oriented but instead more apt to be random and purposeless. It is important to remember that not all children with ADHD are hyperactive.

Impulsivity

Impulsivity is characterized by impaired impulse control and delay of gratification. Children who are impulsive commonly have a hard time waiting and taking turns when playing with peers. They want what they want right now! Children with poor impulse control at times appear younger than their same-age peers. Dr. Russell Barkley, an expert in the field of ADHD, describes children who are impulsive as having no awareness of the immediate past or future (Barkley, 1998). For these children "the next four seconds" are all that they comprehend. Impulsivity makes it difficult for children to think before acting. They often appear to act without planning or considering the consequences of their actions. Activities that require attention to detail are challenging for children who are impulsive.

RYAN, age nine, hears a fire siren and sees the fire truck go by his yard. He is curious to know where they are going. Without thinking that he needs to ask permission to leave the yard and cross the street or that there could be the possibility of danger, he focuses on the sirens and goes. His impulsive behavior and lack of attention to the consequences of his actions, places him in danger. When his parent confronts him and asks why he left the yard without permission or without thinking about his safety, he responds, "I don't know." Frustrating as it can be to hear this, it can be a true statement. Ryan may not be able to explain why he acts without thinking through a situation. ⁑

Additional characteristics that have been observed in young children with ADHD include emotional instability, difficulty interacting with peers, and inconsistent performance. Children with ADHD are more likely to experience minor trauma such as lacerations and fractures than other children. Individuals with ADHD also have positive attributes such as creativity, enthusiasm, and persistence. Some professionals and parents choose to think of ADHD not as a disorder, but simply as a different style of learning. Federal legislation (Rehabilitation Act of 1973, Americans with Disabilities Act, and the Individuals with Disabilities Education Act) recognizes ADHD as a disability.

What Can Cause Attention Deficit Hyperactive Disorder?

In the early 1900s, medical professionals noticed that the symptoms of inattention, impulsivity, and hyperactivity were often seen in children recovering from infections of the central nervous system and children who had sustained some type of head injury. At the time, this condition was called Minimal Brain Dysfunction, Brain Damage Syndrome, or Hyperkinetic Reaction of Childhood.

Now ADHD is one of the most researched disorders in the mental health field. A significant amount of research continues to be done at the National Institute of Mental Health in Bethesda, Maryland. Scientists use magnetic resonance imaging (MRI), positron emission tomography (PET Scans), and electroencephalograms (EEGs) to study the anatomy of the brain. Although researchers have not found one exact cause of ADHD, studies show evidence that ADHD is neurologically and biologically based. Several factors have been identified that appear to play a role in the disorder.

One factor is that of altered brain function. The brain is a complex system and, within this system, there are chemicals called neurotransmitters. Neurotransmitters are messenger molecules that allow neurons (nerve cells) to "talk" to each other, sending messages within the brain. Each area of the brain contains different neurotransmitters. Research shows evidence that the frontal lobes of the brain are the message centers that control activity level, impulsivity, and attention (Jaska, 1998; Jones, 1998; Rief, 1998). The basal ganglia are the area involved in planning complex sequences of action and any sort of ability to inhibit responses. Researchers have discovered that these areas of the brain tend to be smaller in individuals diagnosed with ADHD. Glucose is the main energy source of the brain. The basal ganglia and frontal lobe show a lower rate of glucose metabolism, which indicates a lower level of activity in these areas of the brain. Studies also indicate lower rates of blood flow and electrical activity in the frontal lobe and basal ganglia. According to these findings, researchers believe that there is a deficiency or inefficiency of certain brain chemicals in these

DYLAN was 13 years old and continually frustrated with school. He would come home at the end of the day and have so much pent up anger that it became hard for his mother to face him. Having been misdiagnosed with EBD by the school and sent to the Special Education classroom, Dylan's hatred for school and teachers escalated. He just kept saying, "They don't get it." He began to feel that he was stupid and would say so about himself. His parents didn't know how to approach him because everything seemed to set him off. This situation continued as Dylan grew older, and it was not until he was fifteen that his mom realized that Dylan was abusing alcohol. One night, when Dylan came in really late, she met him. The typical first question to him was "Why?" Much to her surprise, he had a response. "Don't you want me to feel good about myself? Don't you want me to be able to talk to people? I feel great when I am drinking, I feel calm and in control. I am happy and I can talk to people and have fun." All she could do was cry and hug him. He told her that he loved her and not to worry—it would be okay. All the years of raising this child flashed through her mind with pangs of guilt. She knew that she needed help, to help him.

Her first thought was to have him seen by their family doctor. Dylan was given a prescription for Zoloft to help minimize his anxiety and depression. It did not seem to help and Dylan said it made him feel strange. So after a period of time, she visited with the doctor to have him recommend a psychologist. His mother felt that Dylan needed to talk with someone other than a parent—someone more objective. Through proper testing and follow-up counseling, it was revealed that Dylan had ADHD. He was given a prescription for a once-a-day medication that allowed him to become more focused and in control. As a family, they were able to learn strategies and communication skills that allowed all of them to help Dylan become a more "in control" person. This diagnosis opened up a new world of understanding and education and has left their family life changed, but only for the better. Frustrations still come but now they feel they are better equipped to work through them. ⁑

areas of the brain in individuals diagnosed with ADHD. Researchers are currently studying specific chemicals of the brain, one of which is dopamine. Dopamine is believed to be the neurotransmitter that sends messages to the areas of the brain that control movement, regulate attention, and affect motivation.

A second factor that research indicates in the cause of ADHD is genetics or heredity. Children diagnosed with ADHD will frequently have a parent, sibling, grandparent, or other family member with a similar childhood history and behaviors. Experts have found that when a child is diagnosed with ADHD, there is a 25–35 percent probability that another family member has ADHD (Jaska, 1998). It appears that biological factors such as abnormal chemical functioning of the brain are genetic.

Many other possible causes of ADHD have been and continue to be proposed. These possible causes include lead poisoning, refined sugar, food additives, and food allergies. The concept that refined sugar causes ADHD or worsens symptoms of ADHD has been popular, but more research exists that disputes than supports this theory (National Institute of Mental Health, 2010). Food additives such as aspartame, an artificial sweetener, and tartrazine, a food coloring have been studied in relation to ADHD. It appears that these additives may produce behavioral effects but do not cause ADHD. Food allergies may worsen symptoms of ADHD, but there is not adequate evidence to suggest allergies cause ADHD (Wender, 2000; Rief, 1998). There is also some evidence that mothers who smoke during pregnancy, use drugs, or are exposed to environmental poisons/toxins are at an increased risk of having children with ADHD (Mayo Foundation for Medical Education and Research, 1998). Poor parenting, family problems, ineffective teachers, run-down schools, or too much television do not cause ADHD. How a child is raised can affect the severity of the symptoms of ADHD but does not cause the condition. Researchers continue to look at possible environmental factors, and are studying how trauma to the brain, nutrition, and the social environment possible contribute to ADHD.

Diagnosing ADHD

As with any disability, intervention in the early childhood years generally results in greater success and outcomes. Therefore, early diagnosis and treatment of ADHD is extremely important. Early childhood practitioners know that typically developing preschoolers tend to be highly active, distractible, and impulsive. There exists a fine line between the excess or extremes of typical development and the behavior and symptoms of ADHD. This makes ADHD difficult to diagnose during the preschool years. The presence or absence of the symptoms of inattention, hyperactivity, and impulsivity is not the primary issue when concerned that a preschooler could have ADHD. The emphasis must be on the severity and frequency of the symptoms, when the symptoms began, and how the symptoms affect the child's functioning in different environments. Through observation and documentation, practitioners collect detailed and objective information that is valuable in the diagnostic process. Such information includes a description of the child's general behavior, skills observed in various areas of development, atypical behaviors that might indicate a need for further testing, and interactions with peers. When talking with parents about concerns, practitioners need to begin with positive information and identify the child's strengths. Concerns should be shared in the context of the early childhood environment using the practitioner's observations and documentation. It is important to share any environmental and behavioral strategies that have been successful and unsuccessful when used with the child.

Criteria for Diagnosis

The Diagnostic and Statistical Manual of Mental Disorders, Fourth Revision, (DSM IV-R; currently under fifth revision) contains the criteria necessary for making a mental health diagnosis. According to the DSM IV-R, in order for a child to be diagnosed with ADHD, the symptoms must be evident for at least six months and must begin before the child is seven years old. These symptoms must be maladaptive and inconsistent with the child's developmental level. The symptoms also must significantly affect the child's functioning in at least two social settings. For young children, these settings are typically home and early childhood environments.

Three primary subtypes of ADHD have been identified. The names of and criteria for each of these subtypes is summarized as follows.

1. ADHD—Predominantly Inattentive Type

The child must have six or more of the nine symptoms.

- ▶ Often fails to give close attention to details or makes careless mistakes.
- ▶ Often has difficulty sustaining attention to tasks or play activities.
- ▶ Often does not seem to listen when spoken to directly.
- ▶ Often struggles to follow through on instructions or directions given.
- ▶ Often has difficulty organizing tasks and activities.
- ▶ Often avoids or dislikes tasks that require sustained mental effort.
- ▶ Often loses things necessary for tasks and activities.
- ▶ Often easily distracted by outside stimuli.
- ▶ Often forgetful in daily activities.

2. ADHD—Predominantly Hyperactive-Impulsive Type

The child must have six or more of the nine symptoms.

- ▶ Often fidgets with hands or feet, squirms in seat.
- ▶ Often leaves seat in situations in which remaining seated is expected.
- ▶ Often runs about or climbs excessively in situations in which it is inappropriate.
- ▶ Often has difficulty playing or engaging in activities quietly.
- ▶ Often is "on the go" or acts as if "driven by a motor."
- ▶ Often talks excessively.
- ▶ Often blurts out answers to questions before they have been completed.
- ▶ Often has difficulty waiting and taking turns.
- ▶ Often interrupts or intrudes on others.

3. ADHD—Combined Type

The child must have six or more symptoms of inattentiveness and six or more symptoms of hyperactivity-impulsivity.

A fourth subtype is mentioned in some publications.

4. ADHD—Otherwise Specified

The child has prominent symptoms of ADHD—Inattentive Type or ADHD—Hyperactive-Impulsive Type but not enough of the symptoms required to reach a full diagnosis.

Revised from the *Diagnostic and Statistical Manual of Mental Disorders,* Fourth Edition, Copyright 1994, American Psychiatric Association

The diagnosis of ADHD in young children is a complex process because there is no single medical or psychological test for diagnosing ADHD. A thorough diagnostic evaluation is important to complete before beginning any treatment plan. Comprehensive evaluations are important but rarely done. Parents often need to insist that information about their children is gathered from a variety of sources to insure that professionals have the "whole picture" before recommending treatment. The components of a complete evaluation include a thorough review of medical, developmental, academic, and family history.

A detailed, structured interview of the parents is necessary. Parents and practitioners should also complete behavior-rating scales that provide information about the types and severity of the symptoms of ADHD. Intellectual and achievement testing screen for and assess learning problems and help identify areas of strength and weakness. Additional information that is valuable is children's past and present emotional and social functioning, peer relationships, and discipline and behavior guidance strategies used within each environment. A thorough evaluation should take a minimum of two office visits.

Since ADHD can be the result of some medical, psychiatric, and psychological conditions, it is critical that these conditions be ruled out during the diagnostic process. Some of the conditions that can cause look-alike symptoms of ADHD include various learning difficulties, speech/language difficulties, Pervasive Developmental Disorder, Post Traumatic Stress Disorder, Sensory Integration Dysfunction, mood or anxiety disorders, and seizure disorders.

The diagnostic process is also significant because there are a number of disorders that can co-exist with ADHD. Two-thirds of the children diagnosed with ADHD exhibit at least one co-existing disorder. The most common disorders are learning disabilities, anxiety disorders, Depression, Bipolar Disorder, Sensory Integration Dysfunction, Asperger's Syndrome, Oppositional Defiant Disorder, Conduct Disorder, and Tourette's Syndrome.

Who Can Diagnose?
Parents often begin the diagnostic process by scheduling an appointment with the child's pediatrician or their family doctor. The advantage of beginning with one of these professionals is that they have seen the child before and have information about the child's medical,

developmental, and behavioral history. Since preschoolers are difficult to diagnose, it is important that a specialist with expertise in the field of ADHD evaluates them. A pediatrician or family doctor can diagnose ADHD and prescribe medication, but may refer the child and parents to a specialist. Developmental pediatricians, behavioral pediatricians, pediatric psychiatrists, and pediatric neurologists are the most likely physicians to be knowledgeable about ADHD. Child psychologists can diagnose ADHD but cannot prescribe medication. Psychologists and some social workers offer knowledge in other intervention strategies, including individual and family therapy, behavior guidance training, social skill training, and support to children and their families.

Medication

Developing an effective treatment plan for a child with ADHD is extremely important. Clinical experience shows that an intervention or treatment plan that is developed using a collaborative team approach yields the best results. In a team approach, individuals from different areas of expertise share their knowledge and contribute to making decisions and developing intervention strategies for the child. The members of the team are determined by the individual needs of the child. The child's parents or guardians are the decision makers of the team. Other team members may include educational, behavioral, psychological, medical, and social/recreational professionals. Early childhood practitioners are important members of the team. Through observations and anecdotal documentation, practitioners provide information about the child's functioning in a learning environment, his strengths, his areas of need, and how he relates to peers. Educators also make available important information about what environmental and behavioral strategies were used and found to be helpful for the child. When appropriate, the child could be an active team member.

Medications are sometimes used as part of the intervention plan for a child. It is important to remember that medication should be only one component of a treatment plan. Medications are most effective when combined with educational strategies, behavior guidance, parental awareness and training, counseling, and environmental modifications. The interventions used should be specific to children and their families.

Current Information about Medication

Psychostimulant drugs such as Ritalin, Dexedrine, Concerta, Adderall, and Vyvanese are the most commonly used medications in the treatment of ADHD. These medications do not cure ADHD or control behavior but there is evidence they help relieve some of the core symptoms of the disorder. Some experts believe that medication allows children to be more "available" to learn new skills. Medication benefits some children because it helps them succeed in social settings, peer relationships, and in their home environment. Many children taking stimulant medications have been observed to show improvement in attention span, impulse control, regulation of activity level, and ability to complete a task. Researchers have found that these medications appear to help the brain regulate the manufacture, storage, and flow of certain neurotransmitters. It is believed that dopamine and serotonin are two of the neurotransmitters affected. Do-

WHEN a child is physically injured or ill, a parent desires for their pain to disperse. But when the parent cannot resolve the situation, a typical course of action is to take them for medical treatment. There may well be an established relationship of trust with the family doctor and that might be the first place that a parent would turn. But when the issue is behavioral, it becomes much more difficult to seek a proper diagnosis. Often parents will feel guilty or inadequate and be reluctant to air their family problems. But the focus must be the same whether it is a physical or behavioral issue–the betterment of the child's health. Though parents might start by taking the child to their family practitioner, it should not end there, as a psychological diagnosis is the decisive tool. Having the child talk with a psychologist can identify many issues or problem areas. There may be other underlying problems that may look like ADHD but can be something entirely different.

Sometimes parents are confronted by teachers or caregivers who inform the parent that their child has ADHD and needs to be on medication, but this is only their opinion and should not be taken as a diagnosis. ❧

pamine is associated with activity level and serotonin with the sense of well-being.

According to the American Academy of Pediatrics, approximately 80 percent of children display improvements when taking stimulant medications. Generally two or three different stimulant medications are tried before determining that this group of medications is not helpful. There are children who do not respond to or cannot tolerate pyschostimulants. Some non–stimulant medications and antidepressants have been found to be helpful for some children.

The Individual Education Plan Meeting: The Role of a Parent

○ First and foremost, I serve as an advocate for my child.

○ I will educate the team that he is a child first who happens to have a disability.

○ I will remain calm as they list his "problems" and then I'll rephrase them as challenges.

○ I will cooperate with a workable plan by making sure all requirements and obligations on the part of the school are met.

○ I will listen to their ideas and then tell them his ideas.

○ I will check back or request a meeting when I feel that all needs are not met or new ones have surfaced.

○ I will hope that this process helps my child and does not label him or hurt his self-image. ⁑

Mixed Feelings about Medication

Many parents are hesitant to give medications to their children for a variety of reasons. It can be difficult for parents to understand that behavior problems have a physical rather than a psychological basis. Some parents believe that it is easier to fix a psychological problem than a brain that is chemically abnormal. Medical treatment could seem artificial to a parent. Parents also fear that their child will become addicted and/or develop the mindset that medications are always needed to solve problems. Many parents have concerns that their child's personality will change as a result of taking these medications.

Side effects that result from some of the medications used to treat ADHD are also of concern to parents. Common side effects of stimulant medication are loss of appetite, sleep disturbance, and occasionally headaches and stomach aches. A very small percentage of children may develop involuntary muscle movements known as "tics." Tics include eye-blinking, throat-clearing, grimaces, and twitches. Some children become irritable and experience mood swings as stimulant medication begins to wear off. This is referred to as the "stimulant re-

IT WOULD seem to a large portion of the population that there are far too many children and adults on some form of stimulant medication. Many parents do not take the use of medication lightly. They could feel pressure from extended family, friends, teachers, or early childhood practitioners regarding the use of medication. Some parents struggle to come to the conclusion that their child might need a form of medication to help bring some degree of calm and order to their child's life. Often parents can feel guilty if they need the help of medication to alter their child's behaviors. They may also feel that their parenting skills have fallen short.

On the other hand, it can be a relief to some parents who can clearly see that the medication helps their child to be more calm and able to better concentrate. All parents deserve respect and consideration when making these tough decisions. They are the ones who know their child and his behaviors the best. ‡

bound effect." Side effects of antidepressants include dry mouth, constipation, dizziness, confusion, increased blood pressure, and rapid or irregular heartbeat.

Facts about Medications

Stimulant medications were first prescribed for ADHD-like symptoms in 1937. Extensive research and studies have been done since those early years. In fact, psychostimulants have been studied more than any other medications used in pediatrics (Booth, 1998). Evidence indicates that most problems with stimulants are mild and short-term. Stimulants, when taken by adults, create a "high" and when used inappropriately can cause physical and psychological dependence. When taken by children with ADHD, stimulants have a different effect. The children become calmer, less active, their attention span increases, and their impulsivity decreases. Research indicates that children with ADHD do not become addicted to stimulant medications. In fact, emotional difficulties, including substance abuse, are more likely to occur when ADHD is not treated.

Many medications cause side effects. The most commonly reported side effects of stimulant medications are decreased appetite, sleep problems, anxiety, and irritability. Side effects of stimulants often diminish in time. A less common side effect of "tics" or involuntary muscle movements usually stops when the medication is discontinued. Medication interventions should always begin with a trial period. This is a period of time that close observation is given to the time of day medication is taken, specific behavioral improvements, or lack of behavioral improvements. Overlapping times of medication administration can alleviate the "stimulant rebound effect." The child's physician should carefully monitor children being treated with medication. Observation guidelines and checklists for recognizing side effects need to be given to all adults who have significant contact with children beginning medication intervention. Stimulant medications do not change a child's personality when the proper medication is given at the proper dosage. Most physicians follow the "start low, go slow" approach when prescribing medication to young children with ADHD. The initial dosage prescribed is the lowest possible dosage. The dosage is gradually increased until the symptoms of ADHD improve or side effects appear. Based on research evidence and clinical experience, there is no factual basis to support that stimulant medications stunt growth or cause dependence on medication as an adult (Jaska, 1998). Medications are generally only used with preschoolers when their behaviors are so disruptive that they cannot attend child care or a structured preschool.

Medications for ADHD should be administered to young children very carefully. Children should never be in charge of their own medication. Any prescription medications that need to be given when a child is in child care or school are required to be in the original container. The information on this container will provide early childhood practitioners and teachers with the information they are required to have before giving medication. Parents might be asked to sign a medication administration form. Early childhood practitioners are required to record the date, time, dosage, and the name of the person giving the medication. Psychostimulants are "controlled substances" and it is required that any form of this medication be kept in a locked cabinet. When possible, parents might prefer to administer the medication before or after the child care or school. Then practitioners do not have to administer medication.

Young children receiving medication for ADHD should be seen for follow-up visits at least every six months. One purpose of the follow-up visit is to determine the effects of medication on behavior. Parents and teachers provide feedback as to any changes they observe in children's behavior. Early childhood practitioners should document their observations of any changes in the child's behavior or functioning. Other reasons for follow-up visits are to determine the amount of medication needed and how frequently the medication should be given. Physicians should monitor weight, blood pressure, pulse, and request blood tests during a follow-up visit.

Behavioral and Educational Interventions

The optimum treatment for ADHD is a subject of intense debate. Current research indicates that early intervention is a key factor in maximizing positive outcomes for young children with ADHD (CHADD, 2002; Jones, 1998). Medication is only one option of treatment and, as mentioned earlier, most experts believe that treatment with medication is best when combined with behavioral and educational interventions. Psychotherapy gives children the opportunity to talk

about their issues and learn strategies to cope with their symptoms of
ADHD. Clinical behavior therapy helps parents and practitioners learn
strategies for dealing with children's behavior. Family therapy assists
parents and siblings as they deal with the stress of living with children
with ADHD. Social skills training helps children learn appropriate social behaviors. Support groups provide a network of social support,
information, and education for children and parents. Parenting skill
training helps parents develop ways to understand and guide behavior
of children with ADHD. Early childhood practitioners must be aware
of the resources in their community to help parents access necessary
support systems.

Strategies for Success

Inclusion
The Americans with Disabilities Act (ADA) requires that all early childhood programs make reasonable accommodations to include children
with disabilities and developmental delays. An inclusive environment
brings together children with special needs and children who are developing typically. Inclusive early childhood education is based on the
belief that all children are more alike than different. In an inclusive
setting, children learn that people have different kinds of abilities.
They learn to accept and value differences in themselves and others.
Children have the opportunity to develop a wider base of friendships
with other children. Inclusion occurs in public and private schools,
child care centers, preschool programs, Head Start programs, and
family child care programs.

WHEN a person becomes a parent, they want to give everything
possible that they can to their child. They think ahead to their first words, first
steps, and the first day of school. They may even talk about what the child will
become when grown. All parents want the best for their child and it is not any
different for a parent of a child with a disability than it is for a parent of a child
without disabilities. All parents have the same kind of hopes and dreams. All
children want and need to be included as they not only learn from others but
they also have so much to share. Life is a continuing education—for all. ‡

"See What I See In My Child"

I see enthusiasm at its highest as he races in to tell me about a new discovery, rather than a disruptive child who lacks patience.

I see a Winston Cup winner in the making as he sends his mini race cars, accompanied by high pitched squeals, flying across the floor at top speed, rather than an out-of-control, boisterous child who tends to throw things.

I see a budding artist when I look at his homework with extra doodles on the sides, rather than a child who is not focused. Some can do two things at once.

I see a future emergency rescue person or police officer as I witness him propelling himself off the top of the playhouse to feel the rush of risk taking and heroism, rather than a "stupid" child who should know better.

I see the possibility of a carpenter as he takes a pile of boards and builds a clubhouse only to leave the tools lying unattended in order to gather his friends for a meeting, rather than an irresponsible child who won't have another chance to use the tools.

I see a mechanic in the making as I discover his remote control car in an unrecognizable pile of wheels, screws and plastic fenders, rather than a destructive child who won't get another one!

I see a child with hopes and dreams, ambition and ideas, enthusiasm and vitality. He is smart, he can achieve, and he will survive. ‡‡

"Child-first Perspective"

The development of a "child-first" perspective is imperative when working with young children with special needs. The "child-first" perspective places the primary focus on the child rather than the child's disability. All children, regardless of ability, have the same basic needs. Children require that their physiological needs be met. These needs include food, water, and shelter. Children need to feel safe and secure. Children also need to be loved, accepted, and valued. In order to grow and develop to their potential, children need experiences and opportunities to learn. When constructing an environment that provides successful experiences to children with ADHD, early childhood practitioners should begin with strategies that provide successful experiences to all children.

The Early Childhood Environment

Creating a developmentally appropriate environment is critical when working with young children. It is essential that the early childhood environment be designed to meet the needs of all children, including children with ADHD. The physical arrangement of the environment and the social/emotional aspects of the environment influence young children. Learning experiences are developed to meet the needs of all children in the environment. Appropriate environments are created to facilitate children's play, promote cooperative learning, and encourage social interactions.

Physical Arrangement of the Environment. The physical arrangement of the classroom influences how children with ADHD feel, behave, and respond to people and events within the environment. Children are active learners. The early childhood setting should be child-centered and invite children to participate, make choices, and move freely throughout interest areas. Interest areas and activities are based on the interests of the children and provide experiences that build on what children already know. The environment should be well organized, free from clutter, and have limited visual distractions. Children's artwork can be displayed to convey the message that their work is important. Interest areas must be well defined and visible to the adults in the classroom and can be limited to a specific number of children to encourage appropriate behavior. These areas should be arranged to communicate clear guidelines about the activities expected in each area. For example, the fine motor area might consist of a shelf with several sets of small, manipulative toys and a child-sized table with four chairs. This area communicates to the children that four children can play at the table with the toys that are on the shelf. Interest areas often found in an early childhood classroom include dramatic play, blocks, art, books, music, fine motor, gross motor, math, science, and sensory experiences. Each area should be labeled with pictures and words.

The environment should be designed to facilitate play that builds on the positive capabilities, skills, and interests of the children. Play provides children with opportunities to build social, emotional, and cognitive skills. Toys and activities that promote play and interactions with other children are important to include in the environment. Materials and toys available in interest areas must be appropriate for children at different levels of development. Toys that are familiar to the children provide opportunities for them to practice their current skills. Children who have experienced success gain confidence to explore toys that challenge their skills. Play materials and toys for young children with ADHD should be versatile and open-ended. Open-ended toys can be played with in a variety of ways and at varying developmental levels. Toys with bold, contrasting colors stimulate visual interest and encourage exploration. Toys that make noise should have controllable or adjustable sound levels. Storage shelves for toys and materials must be well labeled with pictures and words to promote independence and help avoid chaos at clean-up time. The kinds and quantities of toys and materials in the classroom can have an indirect influence on the children. Having more than one of a particularly popular toy can help eliminate conflicts. All children enjoy "hands-on" experiences. Art materials, puzzles, blocks, and other toys and materials to manipulate need to be included in the environment. Movement activities, music, and sensory experiences also provide "hands-on" learning opportunities. Rotation of toys and materials contributes to making the environment more interesting for young children. New toys and toys that the children have not seen for some time can capture and hold their attention. The environment needs to include at least one soft area using carpet, beanbag chairs, pillows, and other soft materials. A quiet, unstimulating area can be very calming to a child that is over-stimulated.

Schedule and Routines. The classroom schedule is an important aspect of the environment to consider when working with all young children. Most children, and especially children with ADHD, flourish in an environment that has structure and predictable routines. Children need to feel as if they have some control in their world. The knowledge of what is going to occur in the environment can provide children with a sense of control and security. A picture schedule of the day can be a useful tool in communicating this to children. Pictures are used to represent daily activities and routines and are displayed according to the sequence in which they occur. Children and adults can refer to the picture schedule when they want to know "what happens next." A developmentally appropriate schedule includes alternating periods of quiet and active play and periods of indoor and outdoor learning. There is balance of adult-directed and child-initiated activities. Extended periods of time for children to play and engage in projects should be available each day. Children need ample time to explore, learn, investigate, and experiment. Schedules must be predictable and flexible. A schedule that is rigid intrudes, disrupts, and ignores the needs of the children.

The daily schedule should flow at a reasonable pace that enables all children to participate. Plan the daily schedule to avoid a "hurried" feeling. When setting the classroom schedule and routines, it is critical to consider developmental differences in attention span. Most children, who are three to five years of age, can only stay with an activity for a maximum of 10 to 15 minutes. Alternate activities should be provided for children with shorter attention spans.

Giving Directions to Promote Listening. Early childhood practitioners spend much of the day giving directions. There are several important factors to keep in mind when giving directions to all children, including children with ADHD. Most children genuinely desire to please adults and don't ignore directions on purpose. The issue is usually that they did not hear the directions or were distracted while the directions were given; therefore, when giving directions, it is important to get and maintain eye contact. Children are more likely to be successful when directions are broken down into small steps. Directions must be clear and specific. For example, it can be overwhelming for some children with ADHD to hear, "It is time to clean up the room." Instead, make the task manageable and specific by saying, "It is time for us to pick up the blocks. I will pick up the red blocks and you can pick up the blue blocks." When giving directions, it is important to communicate to children what to do instead of what not to do. Using visual cues, gestures, and even simple sign language can be helpful when giving directions. To make certain that directions have been heard and understood, ask children to repeat the directions immediately after being given. Use the names of children to gain their attention before giving directions. A touch on the shoulder can also be used to get a child's attention. Practitioners need to be aware of any child who is extremely sensitive to touch before using this strategy.

Transitions. Transitions are any shift in activities that require children to change their focus or location. Transitions are difficult for most young children and can be particularly difficult for children with ADHD. A schedule that is predictable can be useful in managing transitions. For example, circle time is always followed by washing hands to get ready for snack. Children learn that, after circle time, they can expect to wash their hands and go to the snack table. Early childhood practitioners should plan ahead for transitions that might be difficult by going over the rules, reviewing the behavior that is expected, and letting children know that, although this is difficult, they can do it. Children, with or without ADHD, might have difficulty transitioning out of an activity that they especially enjoy. Giving children advance warnings and time to prepare can ease these transitions. It can be helpful to set a visual timer or a timer that rings to indicate a transition time. Familiar cues such as a song or finger play can be used to signal a transition. Children should not be expected to wait for long periods of time. When a short wait time is unavoidable, do activities and games with the children. For instance, encourage children to imitate your facial expressions, sing their favorite songs, or do finger plays. Transitioning children in small groups, instead of the entire group at one time, can minimize chaos. For instance, "Children who are wearing red may go to the door and find a pair of feet." Different colors of feet can be used to help designate boundaries when lining up. Children find a pair of feet and that is their spot. Children can also be given a responsibility during a transition such as turning off the lights or assisting a peer. Children enjoy being helpers to teachers and peers.

Emotional/Social Arrangement of the Environment. Healthy emotional environments provide security and support the emotional/social development of young children. A developmentally appropriate early childhood environment values individual differences in temperament and ability. Children are encouraged to recognize and express their feelings in appropriate ways. Practitioners who work with young children are available, affectionate, and responsive. Children learn trust and mutual respect when they experience warm relationships with others. Children need to know that they are accepted for who they are, regardless of ability or disability. A sense of belonging is created when all children are given the same opportunities to explore, experience, and participate in the world around them. As children develop skills that help them manage their feelings and emotions, they gain an awareness of the needs and feelings of others.

Behavior Guidance. The goals of behavior guidance include teaching children to identify appropriate and inappropriate behavior, learn problem-solving skills, develop impulse control, encourage empathy, and build self-esteem. Proactive behavior guidance strategies empha-

size the need to be alert, anticipate potential problems, and plan according. Research has identified classroom characteristics that promote success for many children with ADHD. The use of positive reinforcement is one of these characteristics. Positive reinforcement and feedback gives children information and communicates to them what was positive about their behavior. Most children desire and thrive on attention. Although most children would prefer positive attention, the need for attention is so great that any attention, whether positive or negative, is better than no attention at all.

The possibility that children will repeat positive behavior increases when the behavior is rewarded. Many children respond positively to smiles, hugs, affection, and verbal encouragement. Children with ADHD may need extrinsic or tangible rewards such as stickers, a toy, a favorite activity, and others. Rewards need to be interesting and motivating to the individual. Encouragement and rewards must be immediate and frequent. As children's strengths are identified, encouraged, and enriched through positive reinforcement, they are given the opportunity to develop an intrinsic sense of pride and accomplishment.

All children need limits or boundaries for behavior. Expectations for behavior must be specific, clear, firm, and realistic. When communicating limits, distractions must be eliminated so children are able to focus on what is being said. It is important to speak naturally and slowly enough so children hear the limits. Let children know the reasons for the limits. Children should never be told what they can't do without being told what they can do. Giving children choices whenever possible is helpful. Avoid arguing, negotiating, and playing the "why" game.

Active listening, focusing your full attention on what the child is saying, and modeling appropriate behavior are effective behavior guidance strategies. Children develop a sense of trust when their feelings are identified, acknowledged, and accepted. Children learn how to solve problems and control their behavior when adult's model and talk about appropriate behaviors.

Children with and without ADHD do best in a structured environment where they know the rules and behavioral expectations. Children benefit when they know what is expected of them and the consequences that will occur if they chose alternative behavior. Children with ADHD need immediate feedback and consequences for their behavior. Behavioral consequences also need to be used more frequently with children with ADHD. Natural consequences occur naturally as a result of behavior. For example, if a child chooses not to eat lunch, he will eventually be hungry. Discussion and follow-through with natural consequences help children understand that consequences occur naturally as a result of the choices they make. Logical consequences are designed by the adult in the environment and relate logically to the behavior that is inappropriate. For instance, a child is playing at the sand table and is intentionally dumping sand on the floor. The behavior that is expected is that sand belongs in the sand table. The child should be reminded of the expectation and that dumping sand on the floor is not acceptable. He can choose to keep the sand in the sand table or he can choose to be finished at the sand table. If he dumps sand on the floor then he has made the choice to be finished playing with the sand.

Sensory Experiences. Sensory integration refers to the process of the brain that organizes and interprets information received through the senses. The sensory process begins when one of the senses receives information from the environment and sends this information to the brain, where it is processed into a meaningful message or action. Children with ADHD are often overly sensitive to information that is received through their senses. Symptoms of this sensitivity include impulsivity, distractibility, inability to calm oneself, physical clumsiness, difficulty with transitions, and delays in speech/language and motor skills. ADHD and Sensory Integration Dysfunction have similar symptoms and can be confused during the process of diagnosis. The two disorders can also co-exist with one another. The primary goal in meeting sensory needs in the early childhood setting is to assist children to strengthen their basic sensory and motor skills. A second goal is to help children become more focused, adaptable, and skillful. A third

> The family is all together in the living room watching television. The children are told that if they are quiet, they all will be able to enjoy the program. Adam, who is five years old, is curled up in a chair, enjoying the movie when, all of a sudden, a loud piercing scream erupts from his mouth. Mom asks why he screamed. He just looks at her and shrugs his shoulders. He is told to sit quietly, but a few minutes later, he screams again. After a few more times he is told to go to his room. He goes kicking, screaming, and slamming the door. ⁑

goal is to enable children to successfully perform purposeful activities such as climbing, jumping, drawing, and writing. Tactile (touch), vestibular (movement), and proprioceptive (body awareness) activities are useful in alerting, organizing, and calming children with sensory needs. The sensory systems of children who are under-reactive can be alerted by chewing crunchy foods, bouncing on a therapy ball, and jumping activities. Children who have difficulty regulating their responses can organize their sensory systems by eating chewy foods, hanging by their hands from a climber, pushing and pulling heavy loads, or getting in an upside-down position. Activities that can decrease oversensitivity to sensory stimulation and help children become calm include sucking hard candy or frozen juice bars; pushing against walls with hands, shoulders, back, bottom, and head; rocking, swaying or swinging back and forth slowly; and cuddling, big hugs, and firm back rubs. When sensory integration strategies and techniques are part of a child's recommended treatment plan, it is important that early childhood practitioners be fully trained before implementing.

Summary

Attention Deficit Hyperactive Disorder is a biologically based, genetic disorder that affects many children and adults. The primary symptoms of ADHD are distractibility, hyperactivity, and impulsively. The disorder is difficult to diagnose in preschoolers because all preschoolers' display these symptoms at some time or another. A professional, with much knowledge in the field of ADHD should do a thorough evaluation before making a diagnosis. Treatment and intervention plans should be a collaborative effort. Parents, professionals, and other individuals involved in a child's life must work together to develop an intervention plan that best meets the needs of the child.

An inclusive early childhood environment brings together children with special needs and children who are developing typically. Children are seen as being more alike than different. All children have strengths and weaknesses in different areas. Early childhood practitioners must consider these strengths and weaknesses when creating a developmentally appropriate environment. All aspects of the early childhood environment need to be considered in order to provide all children with experiences and opportunities to reach their potential.

Attention Deficit Hyperactive Disorder is recognized as a disability. ADHD does not affect intelligence; in fact, children diagnosed with ADHD are often extremely bright and gifted in certain areas. Children with ADHD have abundant energy and great potential. They are often curious, creative, and artistic. Children with ADHD are not all the same. Each child is an individual with different symptoms, characteristics, and levels of intensity. It can be challenging to meet the needs of children with ADHD in an early childhood program, but it can also be an enriching experience for the children and the adults. Every child enters the program with his very own unique gifts and challenges. The role of the early childhood practitioner is to recognize, embrace, and value each child as an individual that deserves opportunities to learn, explore, investigate, and experience success.

A Parent's Wish List

▶ When he is in school, give my child the opportunity to choose his own comfort zone as to where his desk is rather than being placed automatically next to the teacher's desk. He just might listen better if he is not intimidated by being singled out.

▶ Create a silent signal that can be used for communication between you (teacher or caregiver) and the child so that communication concerning negative behavior can be a silent exchange. He is not comfortable being made an example of in front of his peers.

▶ Please give my child the opportunity to explain himself before assuming that he started a problem once again.

▶ Allow him to hold something during reading time to occupy his busy hands.

▶ Please understand that sometimes directions may have to be repeated more than once. But rather than raising your voice to say the same words over and over, try rephrasing it using different words. We all need a fresh approach at times.

▶ Use pictures for schedules and routines that will help him to organize his tasks.

▶ Respect him as an individual and celebrate his differences.

▶ Join in his laughter and rejoice in the moment. It might be awhile before the next one comes around. Laughter decreases muscle tension and can have a calming effect.

▶ Ask him for his help. It makes him feel important.

- ▶ Embrace each quiet moment and compliment the positive behaviors. It will help him to focus on them more for the gained recognition.
- ▶ Please remember that he is an individual—not his older sister or his younger brother—unique in his own right.
- ▶ Keep him occupied or he will find his own entertainment!

KEY POINTS

1. Children with ADHD display attention issues that can create challenges for early childhood practitioners. Children with ADHD often have a difficult time remembering directions, noises and actions may easily distract them, and concentration can be difficult. The goal of quality early childhood programming is to be inclusive of the needs of all children. Gaining information about different strategies for working with attention issues will help children and adults feel successful.

2. It is challenging to stay up-to-date about current medical information around different disabilities, including ADHD. It is important to learn as much as possible in order to meet each child's unique need.

3. There are many misconceptions about ADHD. Separating what is medically accurate from other perceptions is crucial in early childhood practice to help children reach developmental goals. Sorting through facts and myths can help practitioners better serve children with this disability.

4. ADHD has many characteristics that make it difficult to diagnose. A professional with expertise in ADHD should be consulted by parents who have questions about whether their child may have the disorder. It is helpful to know good resources in your community when referring parents who may have questions about ADHD and their child. It can be difficult for parents to determine to which professional they should turn.

5. There are many external and internal factors that can influence ADHD. A professional can assist parents in finding the best possible approaches to help their child, who has an ADHD diagnosis.

6. To be effective early childhood practitioners need to see the child first and disability second. Finding ways to best include a child with a diagnosis of ADHD can be a collaboration between the early childhood practitioner and parents. Bringing in the expertise of professionals can also be of great assistance in successful inclusion.

7. The DSM-IV is a book medical professionals use when making a diagnosis. It gives them the technical definitions in categorizing a disorder. In the newest edition, there is one disorder that designates ADHD with four subtypes. ADD is no longer a diagnosis. Replacing that label is ADHD-Predominantly Inattentive Type.

8. Not all children with ADHD take medication. For those children who do take medication, Ritalin is the most widely used but other medications can be given. No medication is a cure. When working with a child taking medication, work with the family to determine the best time for the medication to be administered. Families and practitioners often report that children on medication have a "rebound effect" when they are due for the next dosage.

9. Many parents do not take the use of medication lightly. They may feel pressure from extended family or friends regarding the use of medication.

10. A child who has ADHD may need different approaches to learning in order for him to be successful. Practitioners can adapt their programs in many ways to help all children succeed. Strategies may need to be continually reexamined for effectiveness.

11. A child with ADHD may have sensory needs that can be met through using varied play materials.

12. Meeting each learner's unique needs requires imagination and adaptability. Helping each child succeed is best accomplished by implementing a variety of techniques to meet each need.

13. Early childhood practitioners have a great deal to learn from children. They communicate what they need to stay focused during activities and transitions. Practitioners need to be responsive to their cues and adapt.

REFERENCES

Adesman, A. (April 24, 2000). "Does My Child Need Ritalin?" *Newsweek*, *81.*

American Psychiatric Association. (1994). *Diagnostic and Statistical Manual of Mental Disorders.* (4th ed.) Washington, DC: Author.

Attention Deficit Hyperactivity Disorder. (Accessed on February 19, 2002). Available at http://www.mayoclinic.com

Barkley, R. A. (1998). *Attention Deficit Hyperactivity Disorders: A Handbook for Diagnosis and Treatment.* New York: Guilford Press.

Bloom B., Cohen R. A. (2007). *Summary Health Statistics for U.S. Children: National Health Interview Survey, 2006. National Center for Health Statistics.* Vital Health Stat 10 (234).

Brazelton, T. B. and Stanley I. G. (2000). *The Irreducible Needs of Children: What Every Child Must Have to Grow, Learn, and Flourish.* New York: Perseus Publishing.

Bredekemp, S. and Copple, C. (1997). *Developmentally Appropriate Practice in Early Childhood Programs.* (Rev. ed.) Washington DC: National Association for the Education of Young Children.

Booth, R. C. (1998). *Basic Information about Attention Deficit Disorders.* Available at http://www.add.org.

CHADD: Children and Adults with Attention Deficit/Hyperactivity Disorder. (Accessed on February 12, 2002). Available at http://www. chadd.org.

Feldman, J. R. (1991). *A Survival Guide for the Preschool Teacher.* West Nyack: The Center for Applied Research in Education.

Gallagher, Teresa. (February 22, 2002). *Born to Explore! The Other Side of ADD.* Available at http://www.borntoexplore.org.

Gestwicki, C. (1999). *Developmentally Appropriate Practice: Curriculum and Development in Early Education.* Albany: Delmar Publishers.

Glasser, H. and Easley, J. (1998). *Transforming the Difficult Child: The Nurtured Heart Approach.* Nashville: Vaughn Printing.

Gould, P. and Sullivan, J. (1999). *The Inclusive Early Childhood Classroom: Easy Ways to Adapt Learning Centers for All Children.* Beltsville: Gryphon House, Inc.

Greene, R. W. (1998). *The Explosive Child: A New Approach for Understanding and Parenting Easily Frustrated, "Chronically Inflexible" Children.* New York: Harper Collins Publishing.

Henthorne, M., Larson, N. and Chvojicek, R. (2000). *Transition Magician 2: More Strategies for Guiding Young Children in Early Childhood Programs.* St. Paul: Redleaf Press.

Jaska, P. (1998). *Fact Sheet on Attention Deficit Hyperactivity Disorder (ADD/ADHD).* (Accessed on February 12, 2002). Available at http:// www.add.org.

Jaska, P. (October 30, 1996). *Menninger Clinic Seminar: What is ADD/ ADHD?* Recorded on America Online.

Jones, C. B. (1998). *Sourcebook for Children with Attention Deficit Disorder: A Management Guide for Early Childhood Professionals and Par-*

ents. San Antonio: Communication Skill Builders a Division of the Psychological Corporation.

KidsHealth for Parents. (February 12, 2002). Available at http:// www. kidshealth.org.

Kranowitz, C. S. (1998). *The Out-of-Sync Child: Recognizing and Coping with Sensory Integration Dysfunction.* New York: The Berkley Publishing Company.

Kutscher, M. L. The ADHD e-Book. (Accessed on February 12, 2002). Available at http:// www.pediatricneurology.com.

Larson, N., Henthorne, M., and Plum, B. (1994). *Transition Magician: Strategies for Guiding Young Children in Early Childhood Programs.* St. Paul: Redleaf Press.

Lemer, P. S. Attention Deficits: A Developmental Approach (Accessed on February 12, 2002). Available at http://www.devdelay.org.

The Mayo Foundation. (1998). (Accessed on February 12, 2002). Available at http:// www.mayoclinic.com

Medformation: A Community Service of Allina Hospitals and Clinics. (Accessed on February 18, 2002). Available at http://www.medformation.com.

National Attention Deficit Disorder Association. (Accessed on February 12, 2002). Available at http://www.add.org.

National Institute of Mental Health. (Accessed on September 21, 2010). Available at http://www.nimh.nih.gov.

National Network for Child Care: Caring for Children with Special Needs. (Accessed on February 18, 2002). Available at http://www. nncc.org.

Neuwirth, S. (1999). *Attention Deficit Hyperactivity Disorder: Decade of the Brain.* National Institute of Mental Health, Washington, DC: US Government Printing Office.

Paweni, S. N. and Rubovits, D. *The Power of Play.* (Accessed on February 18, 2002). Available at http://www. eparent.com.

Rief, S. F. *Preventing Behavior Problems in the Home.* (Accessed on February 22, 2002). Available at http://www.familyeducation.com

Rief, S. (1998). *The ADD/ADHD Checklist: An Easy Reference for Parents and Teachers.* Paramus: Prentice Hall.

Robertson, A. S. *ADD/ADHD: What Does It Mean for Parents and Families.* (Accessed on February 18, 2002). Available at http://www . kidsource.com.

Sobut, M. A. and Bogen, B. N. (1991). *Complete Early Childhood Curriculum Resource*. West Nyack: The Center for Applied Research in Education.

Special Child: Disorder Zone Archives-ADHD/ADD. (Accessed on February 12, 2002). Available at http://www. specialchild.com.

Strain, P. S. and Hemmeter, M. L. (1997, November). *Keys to Being Successful When Confronted with Challenging Behaviors*. Young Exceptional Children, 2–8.

Wender, P. H. (2000). ADHD: *Attention Deficit Hyperactivity Disorder in Children, Adolescents, and Adults*. Oxford: Oxford University Press.

Wolery, R. A. & Odom, S. L. (2000). *An Administrator's Guide to Preschool Inclusion*. Chapel Hill: University of North Carolina, FPG Child Development Center, Early Childhood Research Institute on Inclusion.

Wrightslaw. ADD/ADHD. (Accessed on February 18, 2002). Available at http://www.wrightslaw.com.

CHAPTER 7

Autism: Including Children with Social, Communication, and Behavioral Needs

Beth Hoeg

A General Description of Autism Spectrum Disorders

Becoming Aware of the Characteristics of Autism Spectrum Disorder

Autism was first recognized clinically in 1943 by a United States child psychiatrist named Leo Kanner. His early description included a definition that from early infancy, children with autism have the inability to form social relationships. One year later, a pediatrician living in Germany named Hans Asperger described a set of characteristics or symptoms similar to those described by Kanner. These symptoms, later named Asperger Syndrome, included social impairment, poor eye contact, limited empathy, difficulty using and interpreting nonverbal communication, unusual or monotone-like speech, an intense absorption in certain topics, and marked resistance to change. Unlike Kanner's description, Asperger's definition did not involve significant delays in language or cognitive development, but did include impairment in fine and gross motor skills. Although described in 1944, Asperger's publication did not reach international distribution until recently due, in part, to the influence of World War II in Germany. Autism, also referred to as Autism Spectrum Disorder (ASD), is now recognized around the world as a developmental disorder of neuro-biological origin that affects brain functioning and usually occurs in the first three years of life. However, how the disorder occurs still remains a mystery under intensive research. In the majority of cases, there is no single identifiable medical, genetic, or environmental cause, although all of these are under scrutiny. Studies show that males are affected four times more often than females, but when females are affected, they tend to have more significant cognitive delays overall.

The term Autism Spectrum Disorder is frequently used to describe the range of related conditions also known as Pervasive Developmental Disorders (PDD). Professionals in the medical and psychiatric field use The Diagnostic and Statistical Manual of Mental Disorders, 4th edition, text revision, DSM-IV-TR, published by the American Psychiatric Association in 2000 to define and diagnosis this disorder.

The Centers for Disease Control describes autism spectrum disorders (ASDs) as a "group of developmental disabilities characterized by atypical development in socialization, communication, and behavior. The symptoms of ASDs typically are present before the age of 3 years and often are accompanied by abnormalities in cognitive functioning, learning, attention, and sensory processing" (CDC, 2007).

Considered to be a life-long disability, autism is described as an uneven profile of development with a pattern of qualitative impairments in understanding social relationships, deficits in communication development, and unusual patterns of behavior, interest, and activities. Some children also experience unusual responses to sensory stimulation such as being bothered by certain sounds, smells, lights, touch, or food textures. Several studies referenced in Cohen and Volkmar's (1997) *Handbook of Autism and Pervasive Developmental Disorders* have shown that as many as 75 percent of people with autism also have cognitive delays, 25–30 percent may develop seizures by adulthood, up to 10 percent could have extremely advanced skills in one particular area, and up to 50 percent might experience anxiety or panic attacks. Autism is often referred to as the "hidden disability," due to the fact that there are no common physical characteristics. However, the impact on the social aspect of development is considerable.

The Prevalence of Autism
Sigman and Capps (1997) previously reported the prevalence of autism as varied, "depending upon how the disorder was defined and diagnosed. Surveys conducted in Europe, Japan, the United States, and Canada reported that the incidence ranged between four and ten autistic children (children with autism) in every 10,000 births."

More recently, the Council for Disease Control (http://cdc.gov/ncbddd/autism) published data from their Autism and Developmental Disabilities Monitoring Network (ADDM), established in 2000, that shows that between 1 in 80 and 1 in 240 children have ASDs. That averages to about 1 in 110 children and an estimated prevalence of about 1% of the population. These results reflect data collected in multiple communities throughout the U.S. during 2006. Health and education records from the communities which participated in the 2002 and the

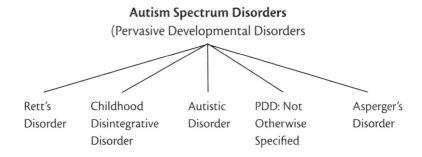

Autism Spectrum Disorders
(Pervasive Developmental Disorders

| Rett's Disorder | Childhood Disintegrative Disorder | Autistic Disorder | PDD: Not Otherwise Specified | Asperger's Disorder |

Joey is a bright-eyed child who is fascinated by the movement of the clouds in the sky on a windy day and begs to go for car rides. He loves to watch the spinning motion of the wheels on his toy trucks. He does not like the noise that the vacuum cleaner makes when his mother does housecleaning, and screams to have her turn it off. His vocabulary for a three-year-old consists of "mama," "NO," "puppa" for puppy, and "eeeaa" for eat. He is very selective about what foods he eats, and refuses to try new foods. Joey's parents describe his first three years of life as challenging and puzzling. He seemed different from other infants from the day he was born. He rarely made eye contact, did not respond to voices and noises around him, and appeared to be deaf. He did not like to cuddle and usually preferred to spend time alone, watching the movement of the fan, the curtains blowing in the breeze, or the circular motion of his wind-up toys. At his two-year-old checkup, his pediatrician suggested further evaluation due to concerns in language delays, lack of social responsiveness, and unusual, non-engaging, repetitive play. A medical diagnosis of autistic disorder was used to describe Joey's unusual developmental pattern. He is now receiving Early Childhood Special Education Services through his local school district. ⁑

2006 prevalence studies were used to conclude an increase in identified ASD prevalence ranging from 27 percent to 95 percent, with an average increase of 57 percent from 2002 to 2006. The Autism Society of America reports 1 to 1.5 million Americans live with an autism spectrum disorder, making it the fastest growing developmental disability.

The total number of students reported on statewide educational child count reports show that an increasing number of students of all ages have met the educational criteria for the autism spectrum disorder category to receive special education services. These increases might not accurately reflect many young children under the age of seven who could have been listed under a more general developmental delay or speech/language category. Therefore, the total number could be considerably higher. Reasons for the increases in the prevalence of autism can partly be attributed to more complete medical diagnosis and educational evaluations, and to a broader and clearer definition of the spectrum of autism in general publications and the media. Early detection is crucial in understanding the developmental differences and to plan appropriate and early intervention for each child.

The average or median age of earliest ASD diagnosis ranged from four years of age to five years, seven months across the country. However, in more than half of the cases, concerns had been identified prior to the age of three years. Lord and Richler (2006) state "it is during this time, between 2 and 4 years, that most children with autism are now identified as having major deficits in social communication, though many parents have noticed differences even in the first year of life." This makes early screening, identification, and intervention more crucial than ever.

Identifying the Early Indicators or Red Flags

Developmental milestones assist parents, early childhood practitioners, and physicians in monitoring a child's growth and developmental pattern. These milestones, or markers of development, show the progress a child makes in her journey to adulthood. While children develop in fairly similar patterns, it is the unusual course of development that draws attention. With more and more information on autism being disseminated, parents, practitioners, and physicians are able to discuss concerns and identify early indicators, or red flags, that warrant further observation and/or evaluation to determine the full extent of the child's unusual pattern of development.

The typical developmental milestones described here include those in the areas of communication skills, social interaction, play behaviors, sensory differences, and motor development. Children under the age of fifteen months should exhibit most of the following milestone markers in their development. If many are missing or unusual in description, it warrants a discussion with the child's parents, who might then take the concerns to their physician or pediatrician.

- Shows an interest in watching faces of people
- Smiles back when smiled at or in interactive play
- Turns toward sounds and to the call of her name
- Shows anticipatory responses such as lifting arms to be picked up
- Establishes eye contact during interactions
- Exchanges back-and-forth sounds with familiar people
- Exchanges back-and-forth gestures such as giving a toy, reaching for a desired item, or taking an offered toy or item
- Uses a few gestures to get needs met (reaching, waving, showing, giving, pointing)
- Imitates the actions of others (tapping hammer, pounding table)
- Plays peek-a-boo, patty cake, or other social games
- Repeats actions that produce attention or laughter
- Makes a variety of sounds like "ma," "ba," "na," and "ga"
- Uses pointing to draw attention to something of interest
- Uses pointing to indicate a wanted item

▶ Begins to combine sounds and words to get needs met and draw attention to something of interest
▶ Uses and understands at least three words, such as "mama," "bottle," or "bye-bye"

Between the ages of 15 and 36 months, children should be exhibiting the following developmental milestones.

▶ Uses many gestures with words to get needs met
▶ Uses at least four different consonants in babbling or words (m, n, p, b, t or d)
▶ Uses and understands at least ten words by the age of 18 months
▶ Understands the names of familiar people by pointing or looking at them when named
▶ Identifies several body parts by pointing or showing on request
▶ Shows interest in other children and plays near or with them
▶ Engages in a broad range of play activities
▶ Uses toys to create simple make-believe play sequences (such as people in a play house going through a daily routine)
▶ Engages in imaginative play (feeding a doll) and looking for attention from a familiar adult
▶ Uses and understands at least 50 words by the age of 24 months
▶ Puts two and three words together in phrases to comment and get needs met
▶ Enjoys playing with other children of the same age in similar activities by the age of 36 months
▶ Enjoys pretending to play different characters with other people
▶ Answers "what," " where," and "who" questions easily
▶ Talks about interests and feelings from past and future events

Parents often consult pediatricians and family physicians with concerns about their child's development. Due to the nature of ASD, parents and physicians must be aware of the red flags that could indicate a child is at risk for atypical development and is in need of further evaluation. The following indicators are adapted from information distributed by Check for Autism Really Early (CARE) (2002) and listed as "Early Parental Concerns" and "Red Flags" which would indicate additional screening or evaluation should occur.

Early Parental Concerns It is important for educational, medical, and early childhood practitioners to realize that parents are usually correct in the concerns that they express about their child's development. If a parental concern is expressed, there is a high probability of a problem in some aspect of their child's development. However, a lack of concern does not necessarily imply normal development. The following parental concerns could indicate a very young child is at risk for atypical development. If a cluster of concerns is noted (any typical child may have a single item on the list), they should be taken seriously, prompting immediate further investigation and routine developmental screening.

Communication Concerns
▶ Does not respond to her name
▶ Cannot tell someone what she wants
▶ Language is delayed
▶ Does not follow directions
▶ Appears deaf at times
▶ Does not point or wave bye-bye
▶ Previously said a few words but now does not

Social Concerns
▶ Does not smile socially
▶ Seems to prefer to play alone
▶ Does things "early"
▶ Has poor eye contact
▶ Is not interested in other children
▶ Is in her own world and tunes others out
▶ Gets things for herself and is very independent

Behavior Concerns
▶ Throws tantrums, is hyperactive, uncooperative, or oppositional
▶ Gets stuck on things over and over
▶ Toe walks and has odd movement patterns
▶ Has unusual attachments to toys (e.g., always holds same toy)
▶ Does not know how to play with toys
▶ Is oversensitive to certain textures or sounds
▶ Lines things up

According to Amy Wetherby, et al, and the FIRST WORDS Project, (Wetherby, 2004), and work by Filipek, et al, (Filipek, 2000) the Red Flags or early indicators of autism spectrum disorders are identified as the following :

If your baby shows two or more of these signs, please ask your pediatric healthcare provider for an immediate evaluation.

Impairment in Social Interaction
▶ Lack of appropriate eye gaze
▶ Lack of warm, joyful expressions
▶ Lack of sharing interest or enjoyment
▶ Lack of response to name

Impairment in Communication
▶ Lack of showing gestures
▶ Lack of coordination of nonverbal communication
▶ Unusual prosody (little variation in pitch, odd intonation, irregular rhythm, unusual voice quality)

Repetitive Behaviors & Restricted Interests
▶ Repetitive movements with objects
▶ Repetitive movements or posturing of body, arms, hands, or fingers

The early childhood practitioner has an important role in assisting families as they sort out concerns regarding the development of their child. The practitioner's role includes:

▶ Knowledge of early indicators, or red flags
▶ Practical discussion with parents regarding concerns
▶ Knowing the referral sources in the local community
▶ Implementing portions of an early intervention plan, if appropriate, as one of the team members

Red Flags or Absolute Indicators

The following are red flags, or absolute indicators, and may indicate a young child is at risk for atypical development. These concerns should be taken seriously, prompting further investigation with screening and immediate evaluation.

- No big smiles or other warm, joyful expressions by the age six months or thereafter
- No back and forth sharing of sounds, smiles, or other facial expressions by the age of nine months or thereafter
- No babbling by the age of twelve months
- No back-and-forth gestures, such as pointing, showing, reaching, or waving by the age of twelve months
- No words by the age of sixteen months
- No two-word meaningful phrases (without imitating or repeating) by the age of twenty-four months
- ANY loss of speech, babbling, or social skills at ANY age

The Identification Process

Understanding the Early Screening Process

The first three years of life are crucial to a child's development. The importance of early screening and identification of possible autism spectrum disorders in young children is critical to early intervention program design and development. Fewer than two percent of all children with a developmental delay or disability are identified before the age of three. In the Minnesota Autism Task Force Report, the following recommendations are given, "autism is a complex and treatable disorder. The identification of autism spectrum disorders, whether made medically or educationally, should be shared with the parent and/or guardian and Individualized Family Service Plan (IFSP) team members as soon as possible. Early diagnosis is critical for appropriate intervention and meaningful outcomes for children with autism spectrum disorders" (Minnesota Autism Project, 2000). The Centers for Disease Control (CDC, 2009) "is working with caregiver and professional groups through the *Learn the Signs—Act Early* public awareness campaign to provide education on the early recognition of signs of

ASDs and other developmental disabilities. In addition, in 2007, the American Academy of Pediatrics recommended that routine screening for autism occur for all children as part of ongoing developmental screening during the 18- and 24-month well-child visits."

Observing Children and Recording Unusual Patterns of Development
Basic screening for autism can occur in a short amount of time. There are a variety of formalized screening instruments published and utilized by both the medical field and educational early intervention teams. With prior training, an early childhood assessment team might use one of the following tools to quickly identify the early indicators or red flags that would warrant a referral for a further multidisciplinary evaluation. These include The Checklist for Autism in Toddlers (CHAT) (Baron-Cohen & Charman, 1996) or the Modified Checklist for Autism in Toddlers (M-CHAT) (Robins et al., 1999) which are designed to screen for Autism at eighteen months of age; The Screening Tool for Autism in Two-Year Olds (STAT) (Stone et al., 1999); the Pervasive Developmental Disorders Screening Test—II (PDDST-II) (Siegel, et al., 2001) for infants from birth to 3 years of age; the Autism Screening Instrument for Educational Planning-3rd edition (Krug, et al, 2008); and the Infant-Toddler Checklist (ITC) as part of the Communication and Symbolic Behavior Scale-Developmental Profile (Weatherby & Prizant 2002). For older children, there is the Social Communication Questionnaire (SCQ) (Lord, 2002); the Australian Scale for Asperger's Syndrome (Garnett and Attwood, 1994); and the Autism Spectrum Disorders Screening Questionnaire (ASSQ) (Ehlers, Gillberg, & Wing, 1999) all designed for children 4 years of age and older. Through a combination of observation and interaction, a physician, psychologist, or educational specialist can evaluate the three core areas of the autism spectrum disorder.

Outside of the formal screening process, early childhood practitioners can observe young children in early childhood settings. Informal notes, data charts, or other incidental records kept by early childhood practitioners should be shared with parents. If parents choose to pursue additional screening or evaluation, they can decide what information to share with a physician, medical specialist, or educational team. Keeping records of behavior and unusual patterns of development can be done in one of the following ways:

1. Writing factual, observational notes in a notebook.

2. Keeping simple data charts to include a column for date, time, behavior noted, length of time the behavior occurred, what happened just before the behavior occurred, and what occurred immediately afterward. (What did the adult do? What did the child do?)

3. Recording how frequently a behavior occurs with a simple tally sheet which would include date, length of time of observation (e.g., two minutes or five minutes), behavior being recorded (e.g., nose-picking or hand flapping) and a column for tally marks.

Sample Record of Behavior

NAME:

Date	Time	Antecedent (What happened) before the behavior	Description of behavior	Length of behavior episode	What happened afterward	Comments

Sample Tally Record

NAME:

Date	Length of observation	Behavior recorded	Total number of tally marks (one tally per behavior noted)

Looking at Medical Considerations

Early screening for ASD can be done through a medical facility or through the educational process. It is a more frequently diagnosed disorder than in previous years, but is often difficult to diagnose due to the variety of characteristics seen from one child to the next. There are no specific medical tests for diagnosing autism; however, a doctor can complete various medical tests to rule out other possible causes or reasons for behaviors associated with autism that could be shared by other disorders. An accurate diagnosis requires skilled professionals to observe a child's communication, social, developmental, and behavioral levels. A medical diagnosis is not required for accessing special education services in the public school setting. However, it can provide a family with a more complete picture of the child's overall development, both medically and educationally, before planning appropriate interventions.

Regular visits to a pediatrician or family physician can provide important opportunities to monitor a child's development and to address specific concerns. First Signs, Inc. is a national organization dedicated to social, emotional, communication, and behavioral development in early childhood. Their goal is to promote healthy development and the early identification and intervention for all developmental disorders, including autism. They have collaborated with their medical advisory board to outline a seven-step process for screening young children. The guidelines were adapted from the American Academy of Neurology and the American Academy of Pediatrics "in order to establish standard practices among physicians, to simplify the screening process, and to ensure that all children receive routine and appropriate screenings and timely interventions" (www.firstsigns.org).

During the crucial period of early development during a child's first three years, children typically make regular visits to the physician. Well visits provide important opportunities to record history, observe the child, and monitor the child's developmental progress over time. First Signs, Inc. has outlined a seven-step process, adapted from key policy statements of the American Academy of Pediatrics and American Academy of Neurology (Practice Parameter)[1], and developed in order to establish standard practices amongst physicians, to simplify the screening process, and to ensure that all children receive routine and appropriate screenings and timely interventions. More detailed information on each of the steps is outlined on the First Signs, Inc. website.

The following screening guidelines for children under 36 months outline a seven-step process for physicians to use when monitoring healthy development[1]:

1. Make clinical observations and chart developmental milestones
2. Conduct routine developmental screening and surveillance

If concerns are raised:
3. Refer to Early Intervention AND to specialist for further developmental evaluation
4. Conduct lead screening
5. Perform formal audiological assessment
6. Conduct autism screening.

If additional concerns are raised:
7. Refer for formal diagnostic testing

The American Academy of Pediatrics recommends that all children be screened for autism at 18 months and again at 24 months by their family pediatrician. They also recommend that treatment not wait until a diagnosis is confirmed, but rather is started as soon as an autism diagnosis is suspected. Their website (http://www.aap.org/) includes a complete list of recommendations. The Centers for Disease Control and Prevention and the National Center on Birth Defects and Developmental Disabilities also provide a wealth of information on the early signs of autism through their *Learn the Signs. Act Early* initiative. Research indicates that there are much better outcomes for individuals with autism when identification and treatment begin as early as possible.

Eligibility for Special Education and Related Services
Children with autism spectrum disorders are entitled to a free, appropriate public education when they meet the state educational eligibility criteria and demonstrate educational needs. A medical diagnosis is not required to meet the educational criteria but provides further information on the whole child. An educational team might include the

child's parents, early childhood practitioner, extended family members, teachers, community health workers, family physician, social worker, or others. The educational team determines, through a team evaluation process, if a child meets the criteria to receive educational services under the special education category of ASD. These special education services are mandated to begin at birth and can be used through early-intervention programs established by the public school in collaboration with various community and county services. A multi-disciplinary team must include a professional with experience and expertise in autism spectrum disorder and knowledge of typical development. Once the evaluation is completed and summarized, the evaluation summary report becomes the foundation for an Individualized Family Services Plan (IFSP), Individualized Educational Plan (IEP), or an Interagency Individualized Intervention Plan (IIIP), all of which serve to address the individual needs of the child. The plan used is based on the child's age and number of agencies beyond the public school that are involved with the child and family. Each plan covers basically the same components but is presented in slightly different formats.

In many states, the eligibility criteria for special education services under the Autism Spectrum Disorders category must address the three core features, which include 1) social interaction, 2) communication, and 3) behavior, interests, and/or activities. Documentation of present levels of performance in each of the core features must also be supported by data showing identified educational needs. Due to the range of characteristics and needs within the autism spectrum and the related clinical or medical concerns, children with different educational profiles and/or a medical diagnosis could be eligible to receive services under the state educational criteria. An effective educational program that addresses the child's strengths and unique educational needs is then planned and implemented. The plan includes the setting and location of services, the service providers and amounts of time, and the methods of instruction and curriculum to be used. Specific adaptations and/or accommodations that might be needed to assist the child to succeed in inclusive settings are also included in the plan. Adaptations or accommodations could be things like the use of a visual picture schedule to help the child understand what will happen throughout the day or the use of picture symbol cards and/or small objects to represent words to assist in communication. Specific teaching strategies such as a structured learning environment or discrete trial teaching techniques could also be used. Another adaptation could include using sensory activities such as jumping on a trampoline for calming, using a weighted vest or blanket for calming, or using headphones to block out noises that disturb the child. Some of these adaptations or accommodations could be appropriate to implement in an early childhood setting and in a home environment.

The Referral Process

Supporting Families

Relatives, friends, or early childhood practitioners could have concerns about a child's development but are uncertain how to bring these concerns to the attention of the parents. As difficult as this might be, it is crucial to pursue any concerns to ensure appropriate early intervention services are started. Generally speaking, early childhood practitioners are in a position of helping children and families but might find themselves in a difficult position of sharing specific concerns regarding a child's developmental profile with parents. However, in reflecting back on those early discussions, many parents have reported to physicians, teachers, and early childhood practitioners that if concerns are suspected, they want to know as soon as possible. As one parent stated "If you know or suspect something isn't right, please let us know as soon as possible. Don't protect us from something we should be aware of and can do something about. We may not like what you have to say, and we may be angry that it is brought up, but in the long run we will learn to appreciate knowing as early as possible."

Disabilities such as autism spectrum disorder appear as a subtle "hidden disability" when compared to those with a more obvious physical manifestation, especially when they are present in very young children. Some early childhood practitioners or clinicians might question if discussing concerns related to autism spectrum disorders leads to labeling a child. As First Signs, Inc. (2001) describes to parents, "a diagnosis doesn't have to be a label. An appropriate diagnosis may describe a child's challenges, but should never define a child." Early identification and intervention enable parents and practitioners opportunities to understand each child as a unique individual and to meet each child's distinct needs to prepare them for adulthood. The goal is to help each child reach his or her full potential. Working with children with autism spectrum disorders and their families in the United States also means, "being sensitive to the cultural context of service delivery" (National Research Council, 2001). This means providing information and services in a language the family is comfortable with and understanding the impact a child with a disability has on a family's cultural context.

Where to Go for Help

Using the Local Interagency Early Intervention Committee (IEIC). In 1986, the US Congress mandated that a range of services, referred to as "early intervention," must be provided to infants and toddlers with disabilities. Public Law 105-17 outlines the provision of specialized services to enhance the development of infants and toddlers with disabilities and to minimize their potential for developmental delay. In many states, early intervention is a statewide, comprehensive, coordinated, multidisciplinary, interagency system that provides early intervention services for infants and toddlers (under the age of three years) with disabilities and their families. Interagency Early Intervention Committees consisted of representatives of county service providers such as human services, public health, and education and community

Early childhood practitioners are encouraged to bring concerns to the attention of the child's parents. In doing so, here are a few Do's and Don'ts that have been offered by parents of children with ASD:

DO:

1. Bring up issues of concern when both parents are present, whenever possible.

2. Start with observations, questions, or concerns of the parent. Be a good listener.

3. Focus on milestones, absolute indicators, and the need to "rule out" other possible causes.

4. Use lead-in phrases such as, "Has anyone brought up the possibility your child may be lagging behind others in communication?" or "When we see difficulties in social interaction, communication and a limited range of interests, we need to refer a family for further evaluation."

5. Put yourself in the parent's shoes. Be supportive, not judgmental.

6. Give specific examples of behavioral indicators that verify your concerns.

7. Refer parents to other medical or educational resources to ask further questions. Be willing to assist in the referral process by offering a list of questions, sharing a summary of concerns, etc.

8. Emphasize the importance of early identification and intervention.

9. Follow up with the family. Check back frequently.

DON'T:

1. Dismiss a parent's concerns. Seek resources together.

2. Scare a parent; keep it positive.

3. Back off from parents who reject the concerns on the initial discussion. If the concerns continue to be present, continue to revisit the behavioral indicators.

4. Assume that bringing the concerns to the parent's attention is someone else's responsibility, or that parents are not ready to hear the information. Objective and informative concerns NEED to be shared with parents.

5. Make assumptions about a support system parents may have; you may be it.

providers such as child care settings, private preschools, and Head Start. The purpose of the Interagency Early Intervention Committee was to continually assess and revise the system of identifying children, ages birth to school age, who may have a delay or disability and be in need of intervention services individually or as a family. A Child Find subcommittee worked with a Public Awareness subcommittee to distribute information about the screening and referral sources available within that county. Individual contact listings were usually listed in a telephone directory under Early Intervention or Interagency Early Intervention Committee.

In 2010, the state of Minnesota implemented a state-wide public awareness campaign to get the word out about the local Interagency Early Intervention Committees. Help Me Grow was established with a statewide information and referral line and online link through the Parents Know website. Minnesota's Help Me Grow: Infant and Toddler Intervention services are provided for eligible children birth to three years of age who may be experiencing delays in their development for several reasons, including special health conditions. These services are designed to meet the unique developmental needs of each child and their family and are offered at no cost to families. Accessing these services as early as possible will ensure the best developmental outcomes for the child. If a parent, family member, early childhood practitioner, or someone from the medical community has concerns about a young child's hearing, seeing, talking, feeding, walking or handling toys, a call to Help Me Grow can be made at 1-866-693-GROW (4769). Referrals can also be made online at the Parent's Know website www .parentsknow.state.mn.us.

Early Childhood Health and Developmental Screening. Many states have passed laws mandating that every child must be screened once before entering school. Local school districts or public health agencies offer this screening for children between the ages of three and six years of age, before a child starts kindergarten. The state educational agency or department sets guidelines for early childhood screening, often in consultation with the state's department of health. Components of the screening include vision, hearing, developmental screening, immunizations review, physical growth, identification of risk factors that could influence a child's learning and a summary interview with parents. Included in the developmental screening might be a parent report and on-site observation by a special education teacher, school psychologist, kindergarten teacher, prekindergarten teacher, registered nurse, licensed physician, or a community volunteer who is guided and supervised by one of the people listed above. Results shared with a parent indicate whether additional referrals and/or evaluations should take place to ensure that a child is developing in a typical, age-appropriate manner. If concerns are noted, a referral for a medical, mental health, or an educational evaluation could be suggested.

Early Intervention Programs. Early intervention programs that serve children with special needs could be accessed through local school districts by asking for the Early Intervention Program, the Birth-to-Three Program, or the Early Learning Program. All of these names describe a set of services that are mandated through the public school system for children under the age of three identified with a physical or mental condition that has a high probability of resulting in developmental delay. These services could include early childhood special education, occupational therapy, physical therapy, speech/language therapy, assistive technology, services from an audiologist or teacher of the deaf/hard of hearing, services from a vision specialist, and/or collaboration with medical personnel and county agencies.

Early Childhood Special Education Referrals. Children between the ages of three years and kindergarten entrance with identified special needs requiring educational services could participate in Early Childhood Special Education services through the local school district. For some children, the transition occurs from the birth to three-year-old programs into the center-based, three- to six-year-old programs, while for others there could be a referral following the early childhood health and developmental screening or a direct referral to the local school district's program from medical personnel, Head Start, community preschool, or family members. Each local school district can direct the referral to the Early Childhood Special Education program.

Accessing County Services and Systems of Support for Families. There are a variety of county-sponsored child and family services available to those families who meet eligibility requirements. Services may range

from maternal and child health programs, financial aid and management assistance, state-sponsored children's health insurance programs, identification of child care resources, mental health collaborative, juvenile court services, Head Start, medical assistance, respite
care, medical equipment, case management, and more. Contacts in local communities are listed in a phone directory under Human or Social
Services and under Community or Public Health Services.

Characteristics of Effective Interventions

A variety of interventions have been developed over the years to assist
families and educators in working with children with autism. These
interventions and strategies seek to enhance the ability of each child
to participate more fully in her environment by improving communication and promoting appropriate social skills. "Rather than attempting to provide a cure, interventions seek to enhance development and
well-being by addressing particular sets of difficulties" (Sigman and
Capps, 1997). Today, in most countries, the core intervention programs for children with autism are educational. These programs might
be carried out in family homes, early childhood settings, or specialized
school settings. Most of these early education programs concentrate
on promoting socialization and communication skills. Children are
taught socially appropriate behavior and how to get along in a group,
and how to generalize skills across various settings and people.

Enhancing the Development of Communication and Language Skills

Communication is more than simply being able to string a series of
words together. "It is the ability to let someone else know that you
want something, to tell someone about an event, to describe an action, and to acknowledge another person's presence; it implies a social situation between two or more individuals" (Layton, Watson, and
Quill, 1995). Research and common practice show that effective communication does not "just happen." Important factors necessary for
successful communication include: understanding cause and effect,
having a desire to communicate, having someone to communicate
with, having something to communicate about, and having a means
of communication. Both the sender (the person talking, signing,
gesturing, or using a communication device) and the receiver of the

communicative interaction (the listener) extend a great effort to accomplish the desired outcome. If either partner experiences difficulty participating in the exchange, the whole process becomes extremely frustrating. Thankfully several techniques and strategies can enhance the success of the communication process. Among these are the use of visual supports and strategies.

Visual supports are defined as "those things we see that enhance the communication process. They are an integral part of the communication circle, enhancing effective receiving, processing, action and expression" (Hodgdon, 1997). Visual supports have been shown to be very effective with children and adults with Autism Spectrum Disorders and with many other language and processing disorders. Rather than verbal words floating arbitrarily into space, visual supports rely on the fact that the information to be communicated is in a concrete, visual form that remains constant. A person who experiences difficulty understanding spoken words might understand the message immediately with the supplemental use of a picture, written note, or sign.

Visual supports may include the following:

1. Body language: Facial expressions, body movements, reaching, touching, pointing, eye contact, eye gaze, position, and distance of the speaker's body in relation to the listener

2. Natural environmental cues: Arrangement of the furniture in the room, location and movement of people and objects, printed materials such as signs, logos, labels, directions, written messages, choices, or menus

3. Traditional tools for organization and giving information: Calendars, daily planners, schedules, shopping lists, signs, labels, maps, instructions, television guides, theater guides, telephone books, etc.

4. Specially designed tools to meet specific needs: Specific picture schedule of daily or weekly events, small picture card used to request a bathroom break, visual timer used to show how remaining time is going away, etc.

Effective visual strategies can be used to provide a young child the opportunity to request something (hand over a picture of a cup to ask for a drink), protest (show an "all done" card to indicate done or no more), or make choices (point to the object or picture when given the choice and the directive "show me" or "choose"). Pictures or objects used for communication should be paired with the spoken words to model the appropriate language for the child.

Using visual structure in setting up the room environment allows the child the opportunity to clearly see how the spaces are defined and what activities and expectations will occur within each defined space. For example, using book shelves, room dividers, or colored tape to mark a border on the floor where the limits of large block building play is to occur, keeps that activity from overflowing into the quieter book corner or housekeeping area. Defining the schedule of the day with visual supports such as a small picture schedule, also allows a child with autism to more clearly understand what will happen next, how long an activity could take, and when the breaks or reinforcing activities take place. All of these supports show a child through the visual mode where things go, what will happen and whose turn it is to do the activity. this reduces the chance of inappropriate behaviors that could result from a lack of understanding and processing the auditory language presented.

Encouraging Social Skill Development in Natural Settings

Most children are born with a predisposition to want to engage in social relationships with people. Infants learn early to elicit and respond to eye contact, social smiles, turn-taking through back-and-forth cooing and babbling, and sharing attention through following eye gaze and gestures. Relationships are formed with familiar people and most young children desire and seek out attention in those relationships. Children with autism spectrum disorders, on the other hand, could often see other children and adults more as a tool to obtain wants and needs, rather than as someone to engage in a social interaction.

Studies of video clips of one-year old birthday parties of children later diagnosed with autism show that even at a young age, the children had a tendency to look up fewer times in response to their name being called, to engage less often in face-to-face interaction with parents and caregivers, and were less likely to follow pointing gestures.

Play skills in young children on the autism spectrum can range from preferring solitary activities, manipulating objects in a stereotyped fashion, or avoiding social interactions of others to the other end of the spectrum where a child could truly want and attempt to interact with peers but not know how to do it. The child could look awkward or odd, may be teased by other children, or may be isolated by peers. The process of teaching social skills and play skills to young children with Autism involves assessing the existing skills, determining what skills need to be taught, how they will be taught, and how the progress toward those goals will be measured. Many of these children do not exhibit typical patterns of development, especially in the areas of language development and social skills. This makes planning goals and strategies more difficult; however, goals fairly common to many children include improving social interaction with adults, initiating and responding to peer interactions, developing appropriate play skills, using communication skills in a variety of social settings to obtain wants and needs, and to request and share information with others.

Suggestions for parents and early childhood practitioners to encourage social-skill development in young children include the following:

1. Maintain a daily routine and structure. Arrange a play space with materials that are visibly accessible and highly organized (using labels or outlines helps with cleanup of materials).

2. Provide visual cues (e.g., gestures, pictures and signs) along with simple spoken language to help the child understand your meaning.

3. Teach appropriate play with toys through the use of imitation (e.g., "Do like me," or "Do this" and model play with the toy such as cars going down a ramp rather than being lined up or pounding the balls into the tunnel holes rather than shaking a hammer and staring at the movement).

4. Reinforce appropriate, positive social interactions such as eye contact, responding to their name, sharing with a peer and initiating a play scenario with verbal praise, combined with either an edible or non-edible item the child prefers. Gradually decrease the use of the additional edible or non-edible item so that the child learns to respond appropriately to the reinforcement that occurs naturally within the social interaction.

5. Set up occasional, structured play situations where peers with typical development are pre-taught the play activity and encouraged to include the child with autism in the play activity (e.g., peers with typical development are taught phrases to use to include the child with autism in a turn-taking game such as rolling the ball back and forth, or playing a table game such as Jenga).

6. Use pictures and a simple story to show the sequence of specific skills needed for success in a particular situation. Children rely on their skill of rote memory and can recall the sequence of the story in needed situations (e.g., "many times children like to play with the same toy. When someone else has a toy I want, I need to use words or my picture card to ask for a turn. I can say thank you to the other person for sharing. I can share the toy with someone else. Taking turns and sharing makes people feel happy").

Guiding Challenging Behaviors

In an effort to provide appropriate programs for children with autism, one of the most frustrating and stressful issues parents, early childhood practitioners, and teachers face is that of guiding difficult or challenging behaviors. It can be extremely difficult to provide natural environments and inclusive settings for children who exhibit behaviors such as destruction of property, physical aggression, self-injury, and tantrums. These types of behaviors can easily isolate or exclude young children from social, educational, family, and community activities.

Conducting a functional behavior analysis can provide critical information that will contribute to appropriate programming (see chapter four for more information). Defining challenging behaviors can be done from a child's perspective or the perspective of the parent or teacher involved with that child. From a child's perspective, challenging behaviors could result from the combination of the inability to understand and process the verbal and nonverbal language in the environment and poor ability to respond or communicate her needs and wants. It may include extreme difficulty in initiating and maintaining social interactions and relationships, which makes playtime frustrating; confusion about how the child's particular behaviors have an impact on others in the environment; and engaging in restrictive and repetitive behaviors and interests that could limit the child's ability to fit in with peers. From a parent or practitioner's perspective, the behaviors can appear to be a lack of compliance with daily routines, tantrums, and destruction of property and aggression toward self or others as a means of control.

Due to the impact of the language disorder on children with autism, many do not develop conventional ways of communicating wants and needs. Although many children display speech and language skills that serve a function of obtaining wants and needs, they may "develop idiosyncratic, unconventional, or inappropriate behaviors to communicate such as self-injurious behavior, aggression, or tantrums. Challenging behaviors are often used to gain attention, to escape from a task or situation, to protest against changes of schedule and routine, or to regulate interactions in a predictable manner" (National Research Council, 2001). It is helpful to look at challenging behaviors from the perspective of the child who may be attempting to communicate something about the situation in a manner that works. Children learn early to repeat a behavior that worked in getting their needs met.

After it is determined that a child may exhibit challenging and inappropriate behaviors as a means of communication, the next step is to identify what may be triggering the inappropriate behavior and what the child is attempting to communicate. Keeping track of behaviors can give information on how often they occur, how long they last, or what happened immediately before to set off the behavior. It can also give information about what may have happened immediately after the behavior sequence, where the child felt a need was met and, therefore, the behavior decreased. Documenting this information can be done in a notebook, using a journal format, or on specifically designed record forms. For example, to record the frequency of a child biting her hand, a chart could have columns that list the date, time, the activity that the child is engaged in at the time, what intervention made the biting stop, and comments.

Looking over this data can lead to some conclusions that might indicate if a pattern occurs such as during a specific activity, around a certain person, or as part of a string of behaviors in a communication attempt. In one such preschool situation, a five-year-old girl with autism spectrum disorders was biting herself and adults who came near her. Upon further observation, it was discovered that the child did indeed have a sequence of behaviors that lead up to the biting, all in an attempt to communicate the need to escape the situation. The behaviors occurred during the unstructured, noisy, free-play portion of the morning preschool schedule. This child began the communication sequence by looking at the door then, looking at an adult several times, trying to get the adult to look toward the door. She then added the word "bye-bye" to the looking sequence, trying to indicate a need to leave the room. The adult with her tried to redirect her to a play area amongst the fifteen or so other children in the room. The child then sat down on the floor and took off her shoes. This brought an adult in close proximity to assist in putting the shoes back on to resume play. However, with the adult close by, the child had easy access to biting the adult on the hand or arm. The adult saw this as severe behavior and promptly removed the child from the room to engage in some sensory activity, calm down, put shoes back on, and return to the preschool setting, which, by this time, had moved through the schedule to a calmer, more structured activity. In looking at this sequence of behaviors, it was clear that the child had difficulty with the unstructured free play, and needed a break. After discussion, with the teacher and assistant, it was decided to take the child for a short walk in the school hallway, get a drink of water, and return to the room after the majority of peers had settled into the last few minutes of play. This allowed the child a shorter period of coping with a stressful situation and gave her a chance to be out of the room during the most hectic part of the play activity. It also greatly decreased the need to engage in inappropriate behaviors because the adults identified the communication sequence and purpose of the biting behavior.

The Individuals with Disabilities Education Act requires that if a child's behavior impedes learning, the educational team must consider strategies and supports, including positive behavioral interventions. These positive behavioral approaches could be implemented and useful in any setting for young children. They are intended to focus on the positive, pro-active approaches that allow the child to be successful in the learning environment. Examples of positive behavioral interventions can include:

Sample Behavior Frequency Record

NAME: **Sally**

Date	Time	Activity child is engaged in	Behavior(s)	Intervention that caused behavior to stop	Comments
5-22	9:15 a.m.	Free play in EC room	Biting hand of adult	Leaving the classroom	Child looking for an escape from noisy, unstructured time. Settled down in hall, had drink of water, and returned when class was settled into routine
5-23	9:20 a.m.	Moving into free play	Biting self on the arm	Going for a walk in the hall	Escape from noise and bustle of classroom moving into free play stations
5-25	9:10 a.m.	Moving into free play	Biting	Leaving the classroom	Escape

▶ Changes in the system, including policies, procedures, staffing, and organization

▶ Changes in the environment, including environmental alterations, schedules and instructional modifications

▶ Skill instruction, including direct instruction to the child and adults working with the child

▶ Behavioral consequences, where negative behaviors are eliminated or minimized and positive, appropriate behaviors are established or increased.

Instructional strategies may consist of using a developmental approach, teaching new behaviors through a variety of research-based techniques, decreasing or altering existing behaviors, using peers as instructors, implementing a variety of visual strategies, or teaching individually versus in a group setting. Other strategies can include using augmentative and alternative strategies for communication such as the use of picture cards to represent words, voice output devices to assist with communication, or sign language. "The expected outcomes from positive behavioral interventions and supports are increases in positive behavior, decreases in problem behavior, and improvements in life-style" (National Research Council, 2001).

Responding to Sensory Needs

Understanding the Sensory System. Autism is a neurologically based disorder that affects a person's ability to process information, communicate, and interact with others. The definition of autism from the Autism Society of America includes abnormal responses to sensations. Any one or a combination of senses or responses can be affected, including sight, hearing, touch, balance, smell, taste, reaction to pain, and the way a child holds her body. The process where the brain sorts and organizes information for appropriate use is the process of sensory integration (Ayres, 1979). It is the ability of the body to receive, organize, interpret, and respond to sensory information received from inside and outside the body.

Sensory integration affects the way a person . . .

- Responds to various stimuli
- Attends
- Learns
- Relates to the environment
- Perceives and uses her body in space
- Relates to other people

It allows a person . . .

- To concentrate
- To organize
- To show increased learning ability
- Academic learning ability
- A capacity for abstract thought and reasoning

Signs of Overload. Signs of sensory integration dysfunction or overload in infants and toddlers:

- ▶ Difficulty consoling self when upset
- ▶ Failure to bring hands together and bang toys
- ▶ Slow to roll over, creep, sit, or stand
- ▶ Difficulty babbling
- ▶ Failure to explore
- ▶ Frequent hand fisting after three months of age
- ▶ Difficulty tolerating prone position
- ▶ Dislikes bath
- ▶ Becomes tense when held
- ▶ Resists being held or dislikes being cuddled
- ▶ Sucking difficulties which make bottle feeding challenging or slow

Signs of sensory integration dysfunction or overload in the preschool child (three to five years of age):

▶ Clumsy, falls easily
▶ Difficulty with balance
▶ Breaks toys easily when playing
▶ Avoids playing with popular toys intended for their age as they may be too challenging and cause frustration
▶ Difficulties in learning to tie shoes, ride a bicycle, and zip or button clothes
▶ Over or under reaction to touch, certain odors, lights, or noises
▶ Dislikes getting hands dirty or going barefoot in grass or sand
▶ Difficulty learning how to use playground equipment
▶ Difficulty with eye-hand coordination activities such as cutting and coloring

Strategies to Increase Readiness Behaviors and Decrease Avoidance and Sensory System Shutdown. There are several intervention strategies that are currently utilized to assist young children with ASD to make sense of the sensory input and messages they receive. Several intervention strategies are briefly described here, and could be recommended for a child and family to be implemented by a specialist or someone trained by the specialist. Sensory Integration Therapy emphasizes the neurological processing of sensory information as a foundation for higher-level skills. A "sensory diet" is where the environment is filled with sensory activities and opportunities to satisfy the sensory needs of the child. Sensory stimulation can also be incorporated through "deep pressure" by using a weighted vest or blanket or through a brushing-and-joint compression program established and supervised by an occupational therapist. Auditory Integration Therapy examines "massaging" the middle ear through certain frequencies of music, which in turn is reported to reduce a child's hypersensitivity to sounds and improve the overall ability of the brain to process and make sense of the sounds in the environment. Vision Therapy includes the use of colored filters, oculomotor exercises, and prism lenses to improve the overall ability of the brain to process and make sense of visual images and how they relate to each other spatially. "In general, interventions based in natural environments that teach or attempt to change behaviors in the context in which they would typically occur have been found to be most effective" (National Research Council, 2001). Helping children with ASD cope with unusual sensory responses within their ordinary environments, or making modifications to those environments, have been shown to be most effective in working through the sensory integration issues. "Children with sensory modulation difficulties may not recognize that they perceive sensory stimuli differently from peers or family. They might not be able to identify what is bothering them or when it is time to take a break. However, assisting a child to put the sensory system in a 'ready state' for an activity may help prevent the negative behaviors and over-stimulation that is part of the child's life" (Mills, 2001).

Planning How to Include Each Child in Daily Activities
Defining the Terms. Looking back to the 1970s, mainstreaming was a popular term used to describe the process of bringing a child with a disability into the mainstream of society. Children with disabilities were given opportunities to participate in activities and educational experiences with peers that were developing typically. In the 1980s, the term integration described the services children with disabilities really needed. This meant that, rather than just sharing portions of the day with peers who are developing typically, opportunities were provided throughout the entire day. Integrated child care received more emphasis as well, as a natural setting for young children to participate in activities together.

Looking at inclusion in broader terms today means that young children with disabilities and children who are developing typically participate together in community early childhood programs. When everybody plays, learns, and grows together, and each child is included in every activity, inclusion takes place. In 2007, the Division for Early Childhood of the Council for Exceptional Children (DEC) and the National Association for the Education of Young Children (NAEYC) began work on a shared position statement on early childhood inclusion to be used nationwide. In April 2009, *Early Childhood Inclusion: A Joint Position Statement of the Division for Early Childhood (DEC) and the National Association for the Education of Young Children (NAEYC)* was officially approved by both organizations. That definition states: "Early childhood inclusion embodies the values, policies and practices that support the right of every infant and young child and his or her family, regardless of ability, to participate in a broad range of activities and contexts as full members of families, communities, and society. The desired results of inclusive experiences for children with and without disabilities and their families include a sense of belonging and membership, positive social relationships and friendships, and development and learning to reach their full potential. The defining features of inclusion that can be used to identify high quality early childhood programs and services are access, participation, and supports" (DEC/NAEYC, 2009).

For a child with a disability to be successfully included into an early childhood setting, much preparation is often required. This may include preparation of other children in the setting, staff training, adaptation of the environment, and possible alterations in the physical setting. Adaptations and modifications to the routine, environment, or activity take daily planning and implementation. Consultation with someone from either the medical or educational field with a background in autism is helpful as well. "Inclusion is a way of providing services that fit a child's individual needs, correspond with the wishes of a child's family, and reflect the unique opportunities that exist within a child's community" (Wolery and Odom, 2000).

Looking at the Role of Peers in Successful Inclusive Settings. Most people in the educational field agree that children with disabilities can and should be included in natural settings whenever possible. One primary advantage is the access to typical role models and opportunities for social interactions that can be found in most early childhood settings. Peers may be taught strategies to include the child in everyday activities such as getting their friend's attention, sharing a toy or activity and talking with their friend. However, for some children or for some portions of the day, the inclusive setting might present too much sensory stimuli for the child to handle. A quiet, individualized learning station may need to be set up. Sometimes, young children may need a longer amount of time working on skills in an individual learning setting until those skills are mastered. Once skills are mastered, the child is then able to take those skills back into a larger group activity or use the skills in different settings and with different people. Overall, there is a general feeling in the field of education that, "educational initiatives should facilitate the child's overall development and aim at allowing the individual to function within as normal an environment as possible" (Burack, Root, and Zigler, 1997).

Summary

This chapter was designed to examine the importance of early identification of autism spectrum disorders in young children. A brief history of autism and a general overview of characteristics and early indicators were described. The prevalence of ASD in school-age children shows an overall increase in the identified numbers during each of the past ten years. Public awareness campaigns through FIRST WORDS Project; First Signs, Inc.; CARE; etc., have increased the awareness and importance of identifying the early signs and red flags of atypical development in very young children, resulting in many more children identified prior to entering school. It is crucial for the medical field and those in early childhood care and education to continue to increase awareness of the early indicators or red flags of autism spectrum disorders in order to locate and initiate appropriate intervention resources. Parents have expressed a desire to have concerns and information shared with them as early as possible. Discussions with families should be done in a professional and respectful manner, with assistance in locating further screening and/or referral sources. A variety of effective interventions have proven to assist children develop more appropriate social and communication skills and have allowed young children with ASD to be successfully included in various age-appropriate community options. Many resources are available both on the web and in print to assist families and early childhood practitioners make wise decisions regarding effective interventions, support, and ongoing information.

KEY POINTS

1. Autism is considered a neurological disorder, considered to be a life-long developmental disability, affecting communication, social interaction, and interests/activities/play skills.

2. Autism has an impact on communication, social skills, and behaviors, interests, and activities. Symptoms may range from mild to severe, and may also have an impact on cognitive ability and motor skills.

3. ASD typically occurs within the first three years of life, affecting males more frequently than females.

4. Early childhood practitioners need to build a successful relationship with parents based on trust and communication for each to share concerns about a child's development.

5. Early childhood practitioners are in a unique position to observe and record unusual patterns in children's development, and to identify red flags that may indicate ASD.

6. Parents and professionals need to be aware and feel comfortable contacting community resources and support systems for children suspected of or identified with ASD.

7. Early childhood practitioners can and do make a difference in the lives of young children identified with ASD when they assist in earlier identification and provision of appropriate early intervention services.

REFERENCES

American Psychiatric Association. (1994). *Diagnostic and Statistical Manual of Mental Disorders* (4th ed.) Washington, DC: Author.

Ayres, A. J. *Sensory Integration and the Child.* Los Angeles: Western Psychological Services.

Baron-Cohen, S. and Charmen, T. (1996). *The Checklist for Autism in Toddlers* (CHAT), University of Cambridge.

Boyd, B.A., Odom, S. L., Humphreys, B.P., and Sam, A.M. (2010). "Infants and Toddlers with Autism Spectrum Disorder: Early Identification and Early Intervention." *Journal of Early Intervention, 32*, 75–98.

Burack, J.A., Root, R., and Zigler, E. (1997). "Inclusive Education for Students with Autism: Reviewing Ideological, Empirical, and Community Considerations," *Handbook of Autism and Pervasive Developmental Disorders* (Cohen and Volkmar, Eds.) New York: John Wiley & Sons, Inc.

CDC. (2009). *Prevalence of Autism Spectrum Disorders.* Autism and Developmental Disabilities Monitoring Network, United States, 2006, In Surveillance Summaries, December 18, 2009, MMWR.

Check for Autism Really Early (CARE) (February, 2002). *A Plan to Improve the Early Screening, Assessment and Identification of Autism in Young Children.* A Report of the Interagency Autism Coordinating Committee to the Minnesota Legislature.

Cohen, D.J. and Volkmar, F.R. (Eds.) (1997). *Handbook of Autism and Pervasive Developmental Disorders.* (2nd ed). New York: John Wiley and Sons, Inc.

Ehlers, S., Gillberg, C., and Wing, L. (1999). "Autism Spectrum Screening Questionnaire (ASSQ)," *Autism and Developmental Disorders, 29*, 129–141.

Filipek, P.A., Accardo, P.J., and Baranek, G.T. (1999). "The Screening and Diagnosis of Autistic Spectrum Disorders," *Journal of Autism and Developmental Disorders, 29*, 437–482.

Filipek, P.A., Accardo, P.J., Ashwal, S., Baranek, G.T., Cook, E.H., Jr., Dawson, G., et al. (2000). "Practice Parameter: Screening and Diagnosis of Autism: Report of the Quality Standards Subcommittee of the Americal Academy of Neurology and the Child Neurology Society," *Neurology, 55*, 468–79.

Garnett, M., and Attwood, A. (1994). *Australian Scale for Asperger's Syndrome.* Queensland, Australia: Griffith University.

Glascoe, F.P., and Dworkin, P.H. "The Role of Parents in Detection of Developmental and Behavioral Problems," *Pediatrics, 95*, 829–36.

Greenspan, S.L. (1999). *Building Healthy Minds: The Six Experiences that Create Intelligence and Emotional Growth in Babies and Young Children.* Cambridge: Perseus Books.

Hodgdon, L. A. (1997). *Visual Strategies for Improving Communication: Practical Supports for School and Home.* Troy, MI: QuirkRoberts Publishing.

Krug, D.A., Arick, J. R., and Almond, P. J. (1979). *Autism Screening Instrument for Educational Planning.* (3rd ed.) Austin, TX: PRO-ED.

Layton, T.L. and Watson, L.R. (1995). "Enhancing Communication in Nonverbal Children with Autism," *Teaching Children with Autism: Strategies to Enhance Communication and Socialization.* (K.A. Quill, Ed.) New York: Delmar Publishers, Inc.

Lord, C. (2002). *Social Communication Questionnaire* (SCQ). Western Psychological Corporation.

Lord, C., and Richler, J. (2006) "Early Diagnosis of Children with Autism Spectrum Disorders" *Social and Communication Development in Autism Spectrum Disorders: Early Identification, Diagnosis, and Intervention.* NY: Guilford Press.

Mills, R., OTR. (Autumn, 2001). "Sensory Issues for Children with Autism Spectrum Disorders," *Educators' Exchange.* Children's Care Hospital & School Leaflet.

Minnesota Department of Children, Families, and Learning. (2000). *Minnesota Autism Project, Promising Practices for the Identification of Individuals with Autism Spectrum Disorders.* Available at www.mnlowincidenceprojects.org/asd.

National Autism Center. (2009). *National Standards project: Addressing the Need for Evidence based Practice Guidelines for Autism Spectrum Disorders.* Available at www.nationalautismcenter.org/affiliates.

National Research Council. (2001). *Educating Children with Autism.* Washington, DC: National Academy Press. National Institute of Child Health and Human Development. Available at http://www.nichd.nih.gov/publications/pubslist.cfm?thegroup=alpha.

Quill, K.A. (1995). *Teaching Children with Autism: Strategies to Enhance Communication and Socialization.* NY: Delmar Publishers, Inc.

Robins, D., Fein, D., Barton, M., and Green, J. (1999). "The Modified Checklist for Autism in Toddlers (M-CHAT)," *Journal of Autism and Developmental Disorders, 31* (2), 131–144.

Siegel, B. (2001). *The Pervasive Developmental Disorders Screening Test-II,* (PDDST-II). San Francisco, CA: University of California.

Sigmann, M. and Capps, L. (1997). *Children with Autism: A Developmental Perspective.* London, Harvard University Press.

Stone, W., Coonrod, E., and Ousley, O. (1999). *The Screening Test for Autism in Two-Year-Olds* (STAT). Nashville, TN: Vanderbilt University.

Wetherby, A., and Prizant, B. (2002). *Communication and Symbolic Behavior Scales Developmental Profile*. Baltimore: Brookes Publishing.

Wetherby, A., Woods, J., Allen, L., Cleary, J., Dickinson, H., and Lord, C. (2004). *Early Indicators of Autism Spectrum Disorders in the Second Year of Life. Journal of Autism and Developmental Disorders, 34,* 473–493. Based on research at the Florida State University FIRST WORDS® Project.

Wolery, S.A., and Odom, S.L. (2000). *An Administrator's Guide to Preschool Inclusion*. Chapel Hill: University of North Carolina.

Recommended Reading

Atwood, A. (1998). *Asperger's Syndrome: A Guide for Parents and Professionals.* London and Philadelphia: Jessica Kingsley Publishers.

Ball, J. (2008). *Early Intervention and Autism: Real-life Questions, Real-life answers.* Arlington, TX: Future Horizons.

Charman, T., and Stone, W., (ed). (2006). *Social and Communication Development in Autism Spectrum Disorders: Early Identification, Diagnosis, and Intervention.* NY: The Guilford Press.

Exkorn, K. (2005). *The Autism Sourcebook: Everything You Need to Know about Diagnosis, Treatment, Coping and Healing.* NY: Harper Collins Publishers, Inc.

Harris, S. (1994). "Preschool Programs for Autism." Austin: Pro-Ed.

Harris, S., and Weiss, M.J. (1998). *Right from the Start: Behavioral Intervention for Young Children with Autism.* Bethesda: Woodbine House.

Harris, S. (1994). *Siblings of Children with Autism: A Guide for Families.* Bethesda: Woodbine House.

Hodgdon, L. (1995). *Visual Strategies for Improving Communication.* Troy: QuirkRoberts Publishers.

Kranowitz, C. (2005). *The Out-of-Sync Child: Recognizing and Coping with Sensory Processing Disorders.* NY: Berkley Publishing Group.

Miller, L.J. (2006). *Sensational Kids: Hope and Help for Children with Sensory Processing Disorder* (SPD). NY: G.P. Putnam.

National Research Council. (2001). *Educating Children with Autism.* Washington, DC: National Academy Press.

Notbohm, E. (2005). *Ten Things Every Child with Autism Wishes You Knew.* Arlington, TX: Future Horizons.

Quill, K. (1995). *Teaching Children with Autism: Strategies to Enhance Communication and Socialization.* New York: Delmar Publishers Incorporated.

Sigman, M., and Capps, L. (1997). *Children with Autism.* London: Harvard University Press.

Teitelbaum, O., and Teitelbaum, P. (2008). *Does Your Baby Have Autism? Detecting the Earliest Signs of Autism.* Garden City, NY: Square One Publishers.

Wiseman, N.D. (2006). *Could it Be Autism? A Parent's Guide to the First Signs and Next Steps.* NY: Random House.

Wiseman, N.D. (2009). *The First Year: Autism Spectrum Disorders. An Essential Guide for the Newly Diagnosed Child.* Cambridge, MA: DaCapo Press.

Minnesota Resources
for Referral and Information

Autism Society of Minnesota (AuSM)

The Autism Society of Minnesota is an organization of families, educators, early childhood practitioners, and professionals committed to
supporting individuals with Autism Spectrum Disorders. Their goals
are to inform and educate families, professionals, and the community
about Autism Spectrum Disorders and interventions that address individual needs, to advocate for appropriate services and rights for people
with ASD and their families, and to support families and individuals
through services and relationships. They can also assist families in various parts of the state with referrals to services that may be needed.

Autism Society of MN 651-647-1083 Fax 651-642-1230

2380 Wycliff Street, Suite 102

St. Paul, MN 55114

http://www.ausm.org

Autism Speaks

Autism Speaks' Family Services helps families maximize their child's
developmental potential and improve their quality of life. They promote and advocate for best practices in treatment, education and all
services—from early intervention to adult care.

www.autismspeaks.org

Minnesota Autism Network

The Minnesota Autism Network consists of roughly 60 educational
staff representing all eleven Planning Regions in Minnesota. Representatives participate in the State Autism Network and are available to
provide technical assistance and training to local districts in all regions
of the state. Their goal is to build capacity of school staff, districts, and
regions by providing assistance with identification, assessment, program planning and implementation.

For technical assistance to schools and to locate professionals with experience and expertise in Autism Spectrum Disorders in specific regions of Minnesota, contact the Minnesota Autism Network. www.mnlowincidenceprojects.org

Child and Teen Checkups Program (C & TC)

Child and Teen Checkups (C&TC) is the name for Minnesota's Early and Periodic Screening, Diagnosis and Treatment (EPSDT) Program. C&TC is a comprehensive child health program provided to children and teens from newborn through the age of 20 who are enrolled in Medical Assistance or MinnesotaCare.

The purpose of the program is:

▶ To identify potential health problems or handicapping conditions;
▶ To provide diagnosis and treatment of those health problems or conditions; and
▶ To encourage the development of good health habits. Contacts can be made through listings in local phone directories under Human or Social Services from the local county.

Help Me Grow / (Interagency Early Intervention Committee)

Contact the state or local Help Me Grow (Early Intervention Program or Interagency Early Intervention Committee) for resources on typical child development and screening/evaluation for young children whose development is not typical. Parents Know website (parentsknow.state. mn.us) gives information on typical child development at different age ranges. Help Me Grow referral number is 1-866-693-4769. Local numbers are listed by County Name and Help Me Grow.

www.parentsknow.state.mn.us

Minnesota Children with Special Health Needs (MCSHN)

MCSHN provides financial support for health care costs of children with special needs.

Minnesota Children with Special Health Needs
Minnesota Department of Health 651-201-5000
   or outstate at 888-345-0823
PO Box 64975
St. Paul, MN 55164-0975

PACER Center, Inc.
(Parents Advocacy Coalition for Educational Rights)

PACER Center is a statewide nonprofit organization that serves families of children and adults with disabilities. Their mission is founded on the concept of Parents Helping Parents, and they provide information and assistance on parents' rights and responsibilities, resources, and legal issues.

PACER 800-537-2237 or 952-838-9000
8161 Normandale Boulevard
Minneapolis, MN 55437
www.pacer.org

Resources

American Academy of Pediatrics
American Academy of Pediatrics is an organization of 60,000 pediatricians committed to the attainment of optimal physical, mental, and social health and well-being for all infants, children, adolescents, and young adults.
www.aap.org

Autism Information in Spanish
Definicion, tratamientos, bibliografia, y organizaciones en Espana (also links to English version)
http://www.autisme.com

Autism Society of America
www.Autism-society.org   800-3AUTISM

Autism Society of Minnesota (AuSM)
www.ausm.org

Center for Inclusive Child Care
A centralized, comprehensive resource network supporting inclusive care for young children in community settings.
www.inclusivechildcare.org

Council for Exceptional Children-Division of Early Childhood
Their mission is to promote policies and advance evidence-based practices to support the optimal development of young children with special needs.
www.dec-sped.org/

do2learn.org
The do2learn teacher site provides free printable learning tools, including picture cards, organizational tools, and information.
www.dotolearn.org

First Signs, Inc.
This web site provides extensive information about typical development of young children, early screening and referral of children with suspected concerns, discussion of treatment options, and links to additional information.
www.firstsigns.org

FIRST WORDS Project
Combined project with First Signs, Inc. to increase awareness of the early indicators and red flags of autism through a web-based video glossary accessible for parents and providers.
http://firstwords.fsu.edu

Help for Babies (0–3) and Educate Children (3 to 22)
Online fact sheets for parents about early intervention and special education services published by the National Dissemination Center for Children with Disabilities.
www.nichcy.org/babies
www.nichcy.org/educatechildren

Help Me Grow
Information for families on typical early childhood development and when to be concerned. Statewide referral number which will be redirected to specific local areas.
www.parentsknow.state.mn.us
1-866-693-4769

National Autism Center / National Standards Project of 2009
The National Autism Center is dedicated to serving children and adolescents with Autism Spectrum Disorders (ASD) by providing reliable information, promoting best practices, and offering comprehensive resources for families, practitioners, and communities.
www.nationalautismcenter.org

Teaching Children with Autism
Favorite teacher tips, information, charts, and strategies
www.polyxo.com

Contributors

DEA ANDERSON has worked with young children and their families for more than 25 years. Dea is currently the Coordinator of Inclusion Consultation Services for Fraser and Center for Inclusive Child Care. She is also working on her Master's Degree in Marriage and Family Therapy with a focus on Play Therapy.

CINDY CROFT is Director of the Center for Inclusive Child Care. She has her M.A. in Education with Early Childhood Emphasis and serves as adjunct faculty at Concordia University, St. Paul, Minnesota. She is an active early childhood trainer, specializing in special needs and inclusion workshops. She has authored "The Six Keys: Strategies for Promoting Children's Mental Health in Early Childhood Programs."

LYNN GEHRKE is an associate professor in the Department of Teacher Education at Concordia University, St. Paul, MN. She currently teaches M.A. level and B.A. courses in elementary and early childhood curriculum, instruction, and authentic assessment. In addition, she consults with public and private early childhood educators in the area of program development and evaluation, curriculum and instruction, and using early learning standards to guide authentic assessment. She received her B.A. (Elem. Ed.) and M.A.Ed. (ECE degrees from Concordia University in St. Paul and her Ph.D. (curriculum and instruction) from the University of Minnesota. She holds a Minnesota teaching license for Preschool and Grades 1–6.

DEBORAH HEWITT is the author of So This Is Normal Too? and coauthor of Play: The Pathway from Theory to Practice and The Optimistic Classroom: Creative Ways to Give Children Hope. She began her work with young children as a therapeutic preschool teacher in the inner city and taught for a number of years in a School Readiness preschool program. She has conducted workshops for early childhood professionals and served on the board of directors of the Minnesota Association for the

Education of Young Children (MnAEYC). Currently she is an Early Childhood Education Specialist at the Minnesota Department of Education.

BETH HOEG is an Early Childhood Coordinator and Autism Consultant as well as a Special Education Coordinator in central Minnesota. Past experiences include 20 years in the field of early childhood special education, as both a classroom teacher and home-based teacher working with infants, toddlers, and preschoolers. She consults with school districts on children with Autism Spectrum Disorder, evaluation, and program planning for children of all ages.

MELISSA OLIVE, PH.D., BCBA-D is the author of 27 peer-reviewed journal articles and book chapters. She has taught assessment and intervention strategies for challenging behavior in young children since 1998. She has also conducted numerous workshops for teachers, families, and other professionals across multiple states. She currently serves as a contributing faculty for doctoral students at Walden University and she manages her own consulting company for behavioral health and development.

COLLEEN PACHEL is a Trainer Support Coordinator for the Minnesota Child Care Resource and Referral Agency and the Minnesota Infant and Toddler Training Intensive Program (ITTI). She is also a trainer, mentor, and consultant for the ITTI Program, the Cultural Dynamics Education Project (CDEP), and Project EXCEPTIONAL MN. In addition, Colleen also serves as an Outreach Resource Specialist for the Child Care Resource and Referral in Minnesota and is the parent of a child with a disability.

CECELIA WESTBY is a faculty member in the Early Childhood Education department at Concordia University, St. Paul, Minnesota. Her primary role is advising and assisting early childhood Master's students in writing their capstones. She also teaches child development at the B.A. level. Ms. Westby has worked in the field of early childhood education for fourteen years as a preschool teacher, center director, and trainer. She has conducted training and taught courses at the University of Minnesota, public school programs, Head Start, and the Minnesota Association for the Education of Young Children.